TEA███████████████████████
✔ KU-533-302

SCHIZOPHRENIA—What It Means

One person is every hundred of our population will suffer schizophrenia before the age of forty-five. One in every four National Health Service hospital beds is occupied by a schizophrenic, amounting to something like 60 000 patients in England and Wales. In addition, several times that number have been diagnosed as schizophrenic but are living at home. Schizophrenia is perhaps the most dramatic and profound of all mental disorders—the one which can result in the greatest long-lasting disability, and which causes the most acute suffering for the victim, his family and friends.

This eminently human and practical book has been written, as the author—a leading Cambridge psychiatrist—explains, 'for relatives who want to understand better, for teachers who want to show their pupils what the real world around them is like, for lawyers who have to battle with the intricacies of the human mind, for priests to whom the troubled go for counsel, for young doctors and nurses who do not specialise in psychiatry but come across madness in their everyday practice and, perhaps most of all, for sufferers themselves—because doctors are notoriously bad at explaining what it is all about'.

Doctors do not know for certain what causes schizophrenia, only that in many cases drugs can control its symptoms. Indeed, drugs have radically altered the patient's outlook: no longer need the diagnosis of this malady imply, as once it did, a life sentence in a mental hospital.

like Sentence of the mind.

71° 199690 — 3

THE AUTHOR

Dr Alexander Ross Kerr Mitchell studied medicine at Edinburgh University, graduating MB, Ch.B in 1958. He began his psychiatric studies at St Francis Hospital, Haywards Heath, Sussex, and obtained the Diploma in Psychological Medicine, and Membership of the Royal College of Physicians of Edinburgh. From Senior Registrar in Psychiatry at Barrow Hospital, Bristol, he was appointed Consultant Psychiatrist to Fulbourn and Addenbrooke's Hospitals, Cambridge, in 1966. He is Regional Clinical Tutor in Psychiatry, and devotes much time to local community and social psychiatry. Dr Mitchell is married, with two children.

EDITORIAL CONSULTANTS

Consultant Medical Editor: Alexander R. K. Mitchell, MB, Ch.B, MRCPE, MRCPsych., Consultant Psychiatrist and Clinical Tutor, Fulbourn and Addenbrooke's Hospitals, Cambridge.

Dennis E. Hyams, MB, BS, MRCP, Physician in charge of the Department of Geriatric Medicine, Guy's Hospital, London (formerly Consultant Physician, Department of Geriatric Medicine, United Cambridge Hospitals; Research Fellow and Lecturer on Surgery, Harvard Medical School and Massachusetts General Hospital).

William R. Merrington, MSI, FRCS, Lecturer and Curator of Museum, University College Hospital Medical School, London (formerly Surgeon, UCH; Research Fellow and Lecturer on Surgery, Harvard Medical School and Massachusetts General Hospital).

TEACH YOURSELF BOOKS

CARE AND WELFARE

SCHIZOPHRENIA
What It Means

Alexander R. K. Mitchell
MB, Ch.B, MRCPE, MRCPsych.
Consultant Psychiatrist,
Fulbourn and Addenbrooke's Hospitals,
Cambridge

With additional sections by

Dr Kenneth Myers, MB, BCh., DPM
Consultant Psychiatrist, Middlewood Hospital, Sheffield

H. Y. Robertson, MA
Clinical Psychologist, Fulbourn Hospital, Cambridge

and

K. D. Armitage
A Senior Social Worker

Foreword by

Christopher Mayhew
Chairman, National Association for Mental Health

ST PAUL'S HOUSE   WARWICK LANE   LONDON EC4P 4AH

Before the beginning of years
There came to the making of Man
Time with a gift of tears,
Grief with a glass that ran.

Pleasure with pain for leaven,
Summer with flowers that fell,
Remembrance fallen from heaven
And madness risen from hell.

Swinburne: *Atlanta in Calydon*

Copyright © 1972 by Alexander R. K. Mitchell
First published by Priory Press Limited 1972
Teach Yourself Books edition 1975

This book is sold subject to the condition that it shall not, by
way of trade or otherwise, be lent, re-sold, hired out or otherwise circulated without the publisher's prior consent in any
form of binding or cover other than that in which this is
published and without a similar condition including this condition being imposed on the subsequent purchaser.

LEEDS BECKETT UNIVERSITY
LIBRARY
DISCARDED

LEEDS POLYTECHNIC

209839

T

58631

ISBN 0 340 19504 5

616.8982

Printed and bound in Great Britain
for The English Universities Press Ltd by
Hazell Watson & Viney Ltd, Aylesbury, Bucks

Contents

Part 3   The Management of Schizophrenia

Foreword

Christopher Mayhew

Schizophrenia is a variant of madness, and madness fascinates us all. Since this is so, schizophrenia should be particularly intriguing because it most readily conforms to the man in the street's concept of 'madness'. The voices, visions and bizarre delusions that lead the layman to label someone as 'mad' are all facets of a schizophrenic illness. It is perhaps the most dramatic and profound of all mental disorders, the one which can result in the greatest long-term disability and the one which causes the greatest suffering for the individual and his family.

For the vast majority of patients the schizophrenic experience is a terrifying and destructive one which leads to progressive deterioration and impoverishes life. It is the greatest single challenge to modern psychiatry and it remains the greatest puzzle.

One in every hundred people can expect to suffer from schizophrenic illness before he or she reaches the age of forty-five. In England and Wales 25 per cent of all National Health Service hospital beds are filled by people broadly diagnosed as 'schizophrenic'. For every one of the 60 000 schizophrenics in hospital there are estimated to be four or five living in the community, getting by as best they can but living greatly diminished lives.

Among those not in hospital are the people we classify as eccentric or just 'odd'; many occupy cells in our desperately overcrowded prisons, still more are the misfits and drop-outs of society—the vagrants, young and old, who make their beds on park benches or beneath railway arches.

Many of the patients who inhabit the 'back wards' of our mental hospitals—the wards which hold out no prospect of cure and in which the atmosphere of despair and human tragedy is overwhelming—are now known to have schizophrenic illnesses. But these people became ill perhaps as much as forty years ago, long before the drugs which can at least keep their symptoms under control were developed, and, by the time the drugs became available, their illness was too entrenched for its relentless course to be altered.

Despite its prevalence and its seriousness there is still little concerted research being done into schizophrenic illness. The name of the illness itself has no precise meaning; it was coined in 1911 to designate not one illness but a group of disorders having features in common. There is still no agreement—indeed, there are fiercely held opposing views—about its origins, treatment and possible cure. Some theories about the nature of the schizophrenic disorder go off into the realms of family dynamics and near-mysticism, while others remain in the complex world of biochemistry. It is a forest of confusion far too dense for the layman to penetrate.

With this admirable book Dr Mitchell, and the other specialist contributors, have cut some pathways through the forest. Now at least the theories and the conflicting views become intelligible. We are presented with the opportunity to review the present state of knowledge and conjecture and to form our own tentative opinions.

The clear thought and impartial information contained in this book is intended for relatives, teachers who are concerned for their pupils to know of the hitherto ignored aspects of life, lawyers, priests and young doctors and nurses in training. But, as Dr Mitchell puts it, the book is 'most of all for patients because doctors are so notoriously bad at explaining what it is all about.'

To become schizophrenic is to become a new person in a new world. This book explains something of that world.

Preface

Schizophrenia has rightly been called the psychiatrist's disorder, for on no other psychiatric subject has so much been written and so many books added to the book shelf. The justification for adding yet another one is that nearly everything else available is written in technical journals or in textbooks for the various professionals concerned with the malady. Schizophrenia is a highly technical subject and if it is to be understood by the lay person, the technical language used by the experts has to be translated into what Wordsworth called 'The language such that men do use'.

Schizophrenia is not an uncommon disorder. It affects about 1 in every 120 of the general population, and about 25 per cent of all the beds in National Health Service hospitals are occupied by patients diagnosed as suffering from it. It is a variant of madness, and madness fascinates us all. We are fascinated much in the same way as a rabbit is fascinated by a snake: madness stares us all in the face and we are terrified that one day we may fall under its hypnotic spell. Madness is all around us in the craziness of the world we live in, in the signs and symbols of art, and madness is inside all of us in our dreams and nightmares, buried away in the deep recesses of our minds.

This book has been written for those who want to know

a little more of what madness, and in particular schizophrenia, is about. It is written for relatives who want to understand better, for teachers who want to show their pupils what the real world about them is like, for lawyers who have to battle with the intricacies of the human mind, for priests to whom the troubled come for counsel, for young doctors and nurses who do not specialise in psychiatry but come across madness in their everyday practice, and perhaps most of all for patients because doctors are notoriously bad at explaining what it is all about.

Alexander R. K. Mitchell
Cambridge
April 1972

Part 1

The Meaning of Madness

'There is pleasure sure
In being mad, which none but madmen know.'

Dryden: *The Spanish Friar*

Introduction

Madness is one of these awkward words that mean different things to different people, and various things to the same person at various times. We use the word *mad* loosely in every-day speech to mean a variety of states of mind: 'he was fair mad about it', meaning he was furiously angry; 'that was a mad thing to do,' meaning that it was a foolish act; 'he was fighting mad', meaning that he was out of control of himself; 'he had gone clean mad', meaning that he was out of his mind; and 'he was real mad about her', meaning he was infatuated.

We have a number of colloquial phrases—'mad as a hatter', 'mad as a March hare' and 'the strength of a madman'. These refer to states of mind characterised by heightened emotion, which lead to behaviour that is unusual, disturbing and potentially dangerous.

We can believe, too, that these various states of mind are due to different things; due to the light of the full moon, due to frustrated love, due to the breaking of various tribal taboos, due to the influence of evil spirits acting from without on the sufferer, or due to some ill-defined internal disruption of vital psychological functioning.

In this book we are concerned with madness in the sense of a person being out of his mind, suffering from a disorder of his mental processes. This is a distressing and disturbing experience for us all, either to witness in others or to suspect in ourselves. Whenever something occurs which is frightening or potentially frightening, we take away its power over us by making fun of it, laughing at it, dealing with it in a familiar way.

Thus we have many slang words and phrases to describe this state, and the mentally disordered person is traditionally the butt of humour and the object of ridicule. We use many euphemisms to take away some of the harshness of the true situation.

We speak of someone being *daft*, using an old Scottish dialect word; *barmy*, which is a word used to describe in other circumstances the frothy surfaces of fermented malt, thus implying that the mad person is full of barm; we speak of him as being a *looney*, a corruption of lunatic, which again suggests the baleful influence of the full moon; we say that he is *nutty*, nuts or off his nut, a nutter or nutcase, using nut as a colloquialism for head: likewise, we talk of him as being *screwy* or having a screw loose; we say that he is *crazy*, meaning broken up; we say that he is *potty* or *queer*; we talk of him as being *round the bend, up the twist*.

All these semi-humorous words hide the stark truth that he is uncomfortably insane and the fear that, if it can happen to him, it can happen to us too.

This protective familiarity extends also to those professionals who are trained to diagnose and care for the mentally disordered; thus the psychiatrist, also the butt of humour like his unfortunate client, becomes the 'nut-cracker', the 'head-shrinker' and the 'trick-cyclist'.

The places where the mad are cared for have been known at various times as the madhouse, the asylum—an honourable old word meaning place of safety—the looney bin and the mental hospital. In the technical literature, even the latter has been transformed into the psychiatric hospital or the unit for psychological medicine.

Man, through the ages, has been haunted by the fear of madness. The old latin dictum was that whom the Gods wished to destroy they first drove mad. Where does this fear of madness come from? Most patients seeing a psychiatrist ultimately come to the point of confession that they are terrified that they are going out of their minds. The fear of madness is not just the fear of loss of self-control, although that is very much a part of it—a fear of losing one's grip, of being taken over by irresistible and incomprehensible forces; the major fear haltingly described is a fear of losing one's identity as a person, literally of losing oneself. Madness is conceived as a labyrinth from which there is no exit and which consists of ever-changing pathways.

The mad person has lost contact with himself, and has lost contact with his neighbour—he is unable to form those relationships from which all else stems. If I am out of contact with myself and cannot contact my neighbour I am truly lost and beyond recovering. The novels of Kafka vividly describe this inexorable process as a person finds himself slowly going out of his mind, with all the terror that goes with this experience.

Many patients state that they would rather be physically maimed than go out of their minds. Physical disablement is visible and understandable. Except in its extreme form it elicits sympathy, but the scars of madness are invisible, incomprehensible and can elicit fear and rejection rather than acceptance.

Ideas of madness are tied up with feelings of guilt, sin, uncleanliness and social ostracism. The mad are therefore to be avoided, driven out, segregated and ignored if they cannot altogether be forgotten.

We talk of the 'happy fool', but this rather condescending phrase is used not to describe the mad person but the witless person, the person who is suffering from mental retardation—the loss of intellect rather than the loss of sanity.

Such persons can be dealt with as innocent simpletons, and the objects of friendly humour. All the jokes about the mad have a bitterness and an irony about them.

Schizophrenia, as we will see later, is a special form of madness. The word has the same basic meaning as crazy, implying that the mind is shattered. The word means literally shattered, split, divided mind—a mind divided against itself. People often confuse schizophrenia with *split personality*. This is a different entity altogether.

Robert Louis Stevenson wrote the novel *Dr Jekyll and Mr Hyde* suggested, it is said, by the life of Deacon Brodie in eighteenth-century Edinburgh. Brodie was an interesting character who by day was a pillar of rectitude, honoured in the city, a staunch member of the Kirk, but by night for excitement he turned to a life of crime as a cat burglar. He was eventually caught and executed for his crimes. In the novel, Stevenson describes a man who has a good and a bad personality at war with each other inside the one body.

Two American psychiatrists in a book called *The Three Faces of Eve* describe a similar situation in clinical practice in which a young girl has two quite dissimilar personalities, one of which does not know of the existence of the other. In her treatment she is cured by the emergence of a third personality which is a healthy compromise between the other two. Such cases are very rare in medicine and have nothing to do with schizophrenia, although, like the schizophrenic, the person certainly can be thought of as mad.

Madness Today

It is difficult to get a consensus of opinion about what such a commonly used word means, but when applied in the clinical context which we describe in this book it can be seen to be applied to disturbing behaviour which contains these three components:

(a) It is inappropriate and incongruous to the person's situation.
(b) It is potentially or actually dangerous to the person or others.
(c) It involves uncontrolled emotions, especially of a violent or of a sexual nature.

If we ask the man on the street who he thinks the mad are, he will say that 'the mad people are those who need psychiatric treatment' because they behave in a way which contains these three components.

An interesting experiment was conducted in America, in which the investigator drew up a series of vignettes of particular forms of behaviour with varying degrees of those three components. These vignettes were then shown to selected subjects who were asked to judge whether in their opinion the person so described was mad or not. It was found that, even with behaviour which was obviously 'mad', th making the judgment was less likely to say the person was mad the more the subject could identify with one person described. In other words, we feel madness is a thing which happens to other people, not to ourselves or to our relatives or to our close friends. The more we can put a person into a 'Them' category as opposed to an 'Us' category, the more likely are we to judge their behaviour as mad if it is different from our own.

So in a sense, madness is not an objective assessment when used by a layman, but rather a value judgment. This has important implications because the law which defines the mad in the context of insanity, and lays down what can be done to them in the way of compulsory treatment, is largely influenced by public opinion, and the majority view as to what is right and proper.

Professionals may try to influence public thinking, but especially on strong emotive subjects like madness, the public mind is as much swayed by deep-seated fears and prejudices as by rational thought.

This natural split in all of us between thinking and feeling lies behind our ambivalent attitudes to madness. In moods of enlightenment we may say that we accept the mad as being just like ourselves and in need of care, but when our emotions are aroused by a threat to ourselves or to those we cherish, we tend to call for stern controls, and what was seen to be an overt acceptance lies (thinly) over covert rejection. This split in us lies behind the euphemisms we use and the jokes which we make. Euphemisms and jokes imply relaxation and acceptance, but they are really a means of hiding the less palatable truth and our more primitive fears.

Attempts at public education in the field of mental health have shown the same tendency to deny reality. In order to overcome feelings of stigma and rejection it has been said 'madness, like all mental illness, is just like any other medical disorder and mental hospitals are just like ordinary hospitals'. In a sense this is true, but only at a very superficial level.

In our thinking we now know that in very important ways mental illnesses are very different from so-called medical illnesses, and psychiatric hospitals operate in very different ways, and are based on very different premises, from non-psychiatric hospitals. In order to make the public less sensitive about psychiatric disorders this kind of educative programme has now led to unreasonable expectations of what psychiatry does and what it can achieve. By making mental disorder, and especially deviant behaviour, respectable the psychiatric services are in danger today of being swamped by ever-growing demands which may not by their very nature be possible of solution in a psychiatric framework alone.

New concepts of the meaning of responsibility and the influence of unconscious factors in the motivation of behaviour have had an effect on the practice of the Police, Magistrates and the Higher Courts leading to a new period of 'enlightenment' which, if carried to the extreme, could mean that the very people who most need psychiatric help and are likely to respond to treatment are crowded out by the growing number of disturbing people who are mad neither in a popular nor in a professional sense but who come into conflict with society and are referred for psychiatric opinion, and if possible for psychiatric management.

As well as this increasing demand for access to the psychiatric services, there is also a reluctance to finance these services adequately because of the underlying ambivalence which we have already described. In an economy where there have to be priorities for the nation's resources, these are likely to be diverted to those areas which evoke the general public's imagination and sympathy. The increasing demand and limited resources result in inevitable frustration, accidents, anger and official enquiries. In recent years there have been two important enquiries based on public unrest about facilities in psychiatric institutions—the care of the elderly (*Sans Everything*) and the care of the subnormal (the Ely Hospital Report).

Contemporary society knows that madness does exist and

that it has to be understood and adequately dealt with, but these deeper emotionally toned ambivalences result in denial, avoidance and, at times of stress, in forthright rejection. Conceptual ideas of what madness is have developed and become more sophisticated, but the underlying and often unconscious emotional attitudes have remained largely unchanged throughout historical time.

Madness in History

Each succeeding age has tried to make some sense of madness, each to its own satisfaction, and if we look at the development of the concept of madness over the ages we can see the historical roots out of which our own attitudes and feelings have grown.

The earliest concept of madness for primitive man seems to have been that of *possession by an evil spirit*. The world was seen to be inhabited by good and bad spirits constantly warring with each other and catching man up in their eternal struggle. A man had to provide for himself maximum protection and took to wearing protective charms and amulets. There were propitiatory and protective rituals to be observed, but all these might fail and he would be possessed, evidence of which was his state of madness. Probably because of the frequent complaint of headache the evil spirit was believed to inhabit his head, and the logical step was trephining or trepanning—making a hole in the skull to let the evil spirit out. Numerous prehistoric skulls exist with evidence of this therapeutic manoeuvre, which was also performed for magical and religious ritualistic reasons—an early connection between things medical and things religious.

Possession is a simple and understandable explanation and occurs in various forms throughout subsequent ages, for example in demoniacal possession—an explanation of witch-craft in the fourteenth century, and the Dancing Mania of the Middle Ages. It is still relevant today in the Voodoo cults of the West Indies and in certain religious cults, such as the Holy Rollers and the Pentecostalists.

Aesculapian medicine in 1250 BC used the principle of possession in the technique of incubation or temple sleep. The patient presented himself and his gift to the temple and after purificatory rites slept in the temple. Aesculapius would appear to him in a dream, offer advice or even perform an operation, and on waking the patient would be cured and would depart marvelling. At Epidaurus in Greece, forty-four cases of successful treatment by this method are described in inscriptions on stone stelae or tablets. All the cases were cured, and the cure was miraculous because the patient had previously been certified as incurable.

This ancient concept of madness contrasts greatly with the approach of Hippocrates, namely that *madness was a form of illness* which could be observed, recognised, recorded and given appropriate treatments. The Hippocratean revolution of the fifth century BC lay in the fact that he insisted on the clinical method: that is, going up to the bedside to examine the patient. Up till then views of illness were based on specu-lation as much as on inspection.

Hippocrates believed that madness was a proper province of the medical man rather than the priest and that, far from the influence of evil spirits coming from without, madness was due to things going wrong inside the patient. Hippocrates was interested in mental functioning and tried to elucidate the relationship of the mind to the body which is still hotly debated in psychosomatic medicine.

From his clinical observations of the patients, Hippocrates recognised three main mental states: mania, melancholia and what was called phrenitis, a condition which we would now classify as delirium.

Early Greek thought was based on the concept of elements, qualities and humours which were in balance in health and ecame disordered in disease. The four elements were air, fire, arth and water; the four qualities, heat, cold, moisture and dryness; and the four humours, blood, phlegm, black bile and yellow bile.

The *humoral concept* of madness persisted in medical thinking from the time of Hippocrates and before, right through to the second century AD when the Roman physician Galen accepted and developed the doctrine of humours. His influence persisted for the next 1200 years unchallenged through the Middle Ages. An excess of a particular humour was seen to give rise to a particular temperament: blood produced the sanguine or optimistic temperament; phlegm the phlegmatic, pessimistic temperament; yellow bile the choleric, irritable temperament; and black bile the melancholic or depressive temperament. This was significant in that it was at least an attempt to classify types of persons and to relate the personality type to internal factors.

The work of modern researchers is in this historical tradition, not relying on humours but establishing somatotypes or body types, and then relating these to the incidence and kind of mental disorders with which these somatotypes are associated.

Dissection of the human body had been forbidden and much earlier medical opinion was derived from dissection of the pig or ape. With the Renaissance, anatomists like Andreas Vesalius examined and dissected the human body. He incorporated his findings in the *De Humani Corporis Fabrica* which he published in 1543. Dissection of the brain and the spinal cord established the normal and the abnormal, and allowed the development of the concept of madness due to *disease of the brain*. This was established as the organ of mind. The subsequent science of neuropathology in the nineteenth century opened up a new era which is still with us—the era of organic psychiatry.

Hans Berger in the 1930s discovered the electroencephalogram—patterns of electrical activity recorded largely from the cerebral cortex. EEG departments were set up in all large mental hospitals. This technique has been invaluable in the elucidation of epileptic disorders and organic space-occupying lesions, but has been disappointing in helping us to understand either the mood disorders like depression or the mental illnesses like schizophrenia.

We live now in the era of the biochemical revolution, with its tremendous byproduct of the vast number of psychiatric drugs. Changes in metabolism and hormones, in neuro-humoural chemicals and electrolytes are now well documented in a number of mental disorders. Many workers believe that the cause of most if not all psychiatric disorders will be ultimately shown to have a physical basis.

An obscure practitioner in eighteenth-century Vienna, Anton Mesmer, is remembered because he introduced an important phase in the historic development of our thinking about mental disorders. He showed that states of altered consciousness and altered behaviour *could be introduced in the subject by other than physical means*. Mesmer was conducting experiments in animal magnetism which were subsequently shown to be questionable, but he showed that a person's wish for an event, his credulity and suggestibility, brought him to a state of mind in which he could be induced to believe that the event had happened.

James Braid working later in Scotland invented the word hypnotism for the technique of mesmerising a subject into a state of altered consciousness by means of repeated stimuli. In this hypnotised state the person could be induced to behave in an odd way and be totally unaware of it afterwards. This showed that others could have power over a man's mind and paved the way for the techniques of psychotherapy—treatment by psychological methods.

If the Hippocratean Revolution was the first major revolution in the history of psychiatry, the second was the Freudian Revolution. Madness was now seen as a *psychological state* without there being necessarily an organic brain lesion. Freud's work was revolutionary but grew out of the work of others. Pierre Janet, Josef Breuer and others were already working in this field, and the great neurologist Charcot was demonstrating the use of hypnosis at the Salpetriérè Hospital in Paris in 1885.

Freud was fascinated by cases of hysteria and studied them together with Breuer. He formulated his great theory of the unconscious aspects of the mind. This became the later basis of psychoanalysis. In dreams and freely associated material, deep conflicts manifest themselves in symbols, and the tensions of these deep conflicts and the counter mechanisms which the mind evolves to deal with them form the substance of madness. It was Freud's theory of infantile sexuality which caused the uproar that brought his work into disrepute, and while a lot of his original work has been modified and developed by the post-Freudians, he made possible a theoretical framework which gives both an explanation of mental phenomena and a technique for dealing with these phenomena when they are disordered.

The concept of the unconscious mind was not acceptable to all psychologists, and in the 1930s *behaviourism* came into vogue. At the end of the preceding century, the Russian neurophysiologist Ivan Pavlov had shown how quite sophisticated patterns of behaviour could be built up in animals using the conditioned reflex.

Conditioned behaviour is based on learning and does not involve unconscious processes, other than saying that the subject is unaware of the learning processes themselves, which are available to immediate study by others. Out of these studies the technique of behaviour therapy has grown: symptoms are seen as learned responses to certain critical stimuli and unconscious processes are not necessary to explain the patient's disorder.

The Second World War brought in what can be called the third psychiatric revolution with the introduction of madness as a function of the relationship between people. This has brought in the era of *social and community psychiatry* through which we are living at the present time. The war led to many psychiatrists leaving the enclosed life of the psychiatric hospitals and having experience of large numbers of people living under stress out in the field. There were not enough doctors to go around to meet the need for individual treatment, and group therapy went some way to meet this need. At the same time sociology was helping us to see how people related to each other and to their social environment. Madness could now be seen as distorted relationships and disturbed patterns of communication.

Family psychiatry was a logical development where the family unit is the group within which the relationships are studied. Social psychiatry has meant that the experience and skill of the psychiatrist have moved away from the study of the individual patient in the hospital or out-patient department to the study of the community at large and to the area where people live. This has meant that this kind of psychiatry is moving away from the traditional medical model and is coming much closer to sociology and anthropology. The disorder has moved from the pathology of the brain to pathology of the interaction.

The medicine of today is not a new creation but necessarily has an ancestry going far back into time. We cannot understand fully what we mean by madness, and disorders like schizophrenia, unless we know how the concepts of today have grown out of the concepts of yesterday.

When we review history from the medical standpoint we can see that many prominent and famous people were truly mad, although at this late date we cannot altogether be sure of the exact nature of the madness from which they suffered. Caligula, the Roman emperor, was noted for outbursts of uncontrollable temper and extreme cruelty. Joan of Arc was a young woman who heard voices and had a vision which others could not share in, becoming a convenient scapegoat for the political forces of the time. In this country George III suffered from an episodic disorder in which his mood changed in inexplicable ways and in which his judgment was so deranged that others had to act for him. Napoleon suffered both from moods of despair and from moods or feelings of omnipotence in which he was convinced he would conquer the world. What is important to note is that, although these persons were at times incapacitated, at others they were capable of considerable constructive and creative effort.

There is a common belief that madness and genius are closely related:

> 'Great wits are sure to madness near allied,
> And thin partitions do their bounds divide.'
>
> Dryden: *Absolom and Achitophel.*

There is also a belief that creative sensitivity may render a person liable to madness. It is certainly true that several creative artists have at times been liable to madness. Robert Fergusson, the Scottish inspirer of Robert Burns, died in an asylum; William Blake portrays in his drawings experiences of a mad world; the composer Robert Schumann suffered from insanity; and the story of Van Gogh cutting off his ear in a fit of despair is well known.

Madness in Art

The relationship between sensitivity, creativity and madness is a very interesting one. The creative artist is one who is sensitive enough both to register the quality of his own experience and to record it in such a way that others may meaningfully share in that experience. The creativity arises directly out of the sensitivity, but sensitivity renders the subject more capable of suffering, which in an extreme results in madness if the psychic defences are inadequate to cope with it. It should also be noted that madness can release creativity, in that during a period of madness artists have been known to produce an exciting quality of work which is not to be re-captured once the mad episode is over. It is equally true, of course, that madness can also interrupt and destroy a creative stream.

Other artists, not themselves necessarily mad, have sought to reflect in their work the fascinating aspects of the experience of madness. Writers like Kafka, Dostoevsky and William Joyce open up the world of fantasy, but also the world of entanglement and estrangement, and in particular the Marquis de Sade and von Sacher-Masoch explore the world of perverted sexuality. The visual arts abound in examples of representation of the world of fear and fantasy—Hieronymus Bosch and Albrecht Dürer show us visions of a world as horrific as any schizophrenic hallucinatory experience, and modern artists like Picasso and Salvador Dali make frequent use of visual fantasy built upon symbols which are also found in the dreams of the mad. In sound it is less easy to portray explicitly disintegration and degradation, but one can think of the *Symphonie Fantastique* of Hector Berlioz and the hectic frenzy of Stravinsky's *Rite of Spring*.

Art which seeks to recreate the world of madness can be incomprehensible and apparently uncontrolled in the way it contravenes established rules. It freely uses fantasy and conjures up symbols of the unconscious. It is disturbing to the spectator because of its portrayal of the world of hidden fears. The emotions of fear and anxiety which it evokes in us are the vehicle whereby we remain fascinated and repelled by it in one and the same moment, just as we are both fascinated and repelled by the mad themselves.

Madness and Insanity

Questions of madness take us into the legal world where the issue of responsibility is frequently at stake. Before a person can be judged on an act and punished for it if it breaks the law, he must be shown to be responsible for it. That means that he must be shown to be accountable for the act, to be aware of the difference between right and wrong, and to be operating in a moral framework congruous with that of society as a whole.

Insanity is essentially a legal concept and implies that the person is not responsible for his actions or a particular action by reason of *non mens rea*—not being in his right mind. This means that he is judged not to be capable of making valid judgments about himself or others.

Mental illness, on the other hand, is a medical concept and implies that the person is suffering from an illness of his mind which may or may not affect his ability to make valid judgments. Thus although being mentally ill, he may not necessarily be legally insane.

Insanity places emphasis on the cognitive functions primarily, that is knowing who he is, knowing what he is doing and knowing whether it is right or wrong, whereas mental illness is concerned not only with what a man thinks but, more important, with what he feels. The law treats man as a sentient being until proved otherwise, but medicine is aware that the motivations for behaviour are as often unconscious and stem from deep feelings as from conscious controlled rational thoughts.

This difference in concept has been highlighted by a famous legal instrument—the McNaghten Rules. These were devised after the trial in 1843 of Daniel McNaghten, who in a fit of madness attempted to murder Sir Robert Peel.* The Rules, used in cases of murder, asked whether the accused knew what he was doing and, if he did, whether he knew it was wrong. These Rules have largely been superseded by the Homicide Act 1957, which recognises the power of human emotion in determining behaviour and allows the plea of diminished responsibility.

The question of the irresistible impulse has always been a difficult one to assess. Because a feeling is very strong does not necessarily mean that it cannot be resisted.

The importance of all this for the mad person is that if by reason of mental illness he is operating from a different frame of reference as the rest of society because of delusional thinking and disturbed emotion, he may not be able to plead or to instruct his defence, and may not be responsible for his actions as already described. If it is subsequently shown that he did commit a felony, he should then be dealt with in a manner different from that of another person deemed to be sane. The basic question is whether he is bad or mad. The principle would seem to be that if he is bad he should be punished and if he is mad he should be treated. However, it is rarely as simple as that because people can be mad and bad at the same time with varying degrees of each condition present. The disposal of the person then depends on judging the exact degree of each condition and organising his care in the direction dictated by the major one.

In passing, it should be noted that the word *lunacy* has an ancient history. It perpetuates the idea that madness is in some

* But killed his Private Secretary instead.

way linked to phases of the moon. Milton in *Paradise Lost* speaks of

> 'Demoniac frenzy, moping melancholy,
> And moon-struck madness.'

The word was incorporated into medical usage to describe the institutions where the mad people were cared for, the lunatic asylums, and was also used in the official legislature of the time which defined the statutory care of such people—the Lunacy Acts. Lunacy therefore has a more medical connotation than madness but a less judicial one than insanity.

Madness and Psychiatry

Psychiatry is that branch of medicine which deals with abnormal behaviour arising from mental disorders. Because human reactions to stress and frustration are so varied, it has been helpful to divide mental disorders into two main groups:

(a) *the neuroses (psychoneuroses),*
(b) *the psychoses.*

The neuroses are classified as the minor mental disorders which show a disturbance mainly in the field of the patient's feelings.

These disorders are characterised by fears, anxieties, tensions, guilts and interpersonal conflicts, which are often related to specific circumstances: for example, fear of going into crowded places. In other situations, however, there apparently is no obvious cause for the patient's symptoms and this in itself is a further source of anxiety. The neurotic patient remains in contact with reality, and because his reasoning powers remain intact he is usually able to continue to function adequately until he reaches a particular emotional breaking point.

The psychoses are classified as the major mental disorders which involve the thinking as well as the feeling of the patient. His judgment becomes impaired and he is unable to perceive clearly his particular situation and his relationship to those around him. As a result the patient is liable to lose contact with reality and ceases to be able to function in any meaningful way.

This is a very simple classification, but it helps us to see into which category a patient generally fits. The importance of this is to ascertain his ability to continue in the community, the treatment which he requires and the likely outcome of his disorder.

We can now see that 'madness' is a somewhat imprecise term used loosely to describe behaviour which in a more technical sense would be classified with the group of the psychoses. Madness in psychiatric language is therefore a psychotic condition.

The psychoses themselves are a complex group of serious mental disorders which again can be subdivided into:

(a) *the organic psychoses,*
(b) *the functional psychoses.*

The organic psychoses are those disorders due to a disease process which has physical effects on the brain. Physical effects can be quite gross, as for example when there is a cerebral tumour, but they can also operate at a microscopic or cellular level, as for example in states of chemical intoxication. Whatever the cause of the organic psychosis there is usually at some stage of the disorder an effect on consciousness, so that the patient may be unconscious or have a fluctuating awareness of what is going on round him. This is called clouding of consciousness.

The functional psychoses are not due to any easily demonstrable change in the brain but are believed to be due to a major disturbance of function rather than structure. Modern research shows that there may be a disorder at the chemical level in some cases of functional psychoses, but not necessarily in all of them.

The functional psychoses once more are subdivided into:

(a) *manic depressive psychosis*—a disorder characterised by extreme fluctuations of mood,

(b) *schizophrenia*—a disorder affecting all modes of psychic function.

We can now see schizophrenia in its proper perspective—it is a variant of madness, a psychotic condition, placed in the group of functional psychoses.

Part 2

What is Schizophrenia

'*Quem Juppiter vult perdere, dementat prius.*'
'Whom the Gods wish to destroy, they first drive mad.'

Latin dictum

Introduction

Having looked at the meanings of words like *madness*, *insanity* and *lunacy*, and having defined the place of schizophrenia within the study of psychiatry, we should now examine the nature of schizophrenia in general. This can be done from two viewpoints.

First, from that of the external observer who wishes to study schizophrenia in the medical, psychological and social context —in other words, from that of the observer who wishes to ask what kind of disorder schizophrenia is, what are its causes and how is it to be recognised in its clinical manifestations. The second viewpoint is the internal subjective viewpoint of the schizophrenic himself, asking such questions as 'What does it feel like to be schizophrenic?' and 'How does the world of others appear from the patient's position?' This is a study of phenomenology which seeks to explore the inner world of the schizophrenic experience.

For a long time it was thought that the first approach was sufficient for the scientific understanding of such a disorder as schizophrenia, but now we know that an approach which only seeks to define a disorder in terms of how it appears to others, and omits a consideration of the quality of the experience of living through that disorder, can only give a partial account of the nature of the subject under discussion.

The concept of schizophrenia

When the seriously mentally disordered were gathered together into institutions such as the early private madhouses, the first classifications of patients separated out subgroups based on the clinical behaviour of the patients and the course of their disorders. In 1860 Morel described a condition which he called *Démence précoce* which was characterised by intellectual deterioration in adolescent patients for no apparent reason. This was to be distinguished from conditions in which intellectual development had never occurred or had halted at a particular age, the condition now known as subnormality or mental retardation. Morel's patients had developed normally but in the late adolescent period began to show a progressive loss of intellectual function which appeared then to be irreversible. Following on this work, the great descriptive psychiatrist Kraepelin used the term *Dementia Praecox* to describe a group of illnesses occurring in young people, and all characterised by progressive intellectual deterioration. The Swiss psychiatrist Eugen Bleuler then published in 1911 a famous monograph entitled *The Schizophrenias*—'By the term schizophrenia we designate a group of psychoses whose course is at times chronic, at times marked by intermittent attacks and which can stop or retrograde at any given stage, but does not permit a full *restitutio ad integrum*. The disease is characterised by a specific type of thinking, feeling and relation to the external world which appears nowhere else in this particular fashion.'

As well as describing the condition in considerable detail and suggesting possible causations, Bleuler made the fundamental contribution of recognising that this was not one discreet illness, but a group of disorders having many features in common. In the light of this approach the question 'What is the cause of schizophrenia?' becomes meaningless, and has to be rephrased into something like 'What are the various causes of the group of disorders which we recognise as the schizophrenias?'

The difficulty of finding an agreed operant definition of what is exactly meant by 'schizophrenia' has hampered basic research into its causations, and accounts for some of the confusion and wildly differing views held at the present time. Thomas Szasz, an American psychiatrist, has pointed out that there are dangerous words called panchrestons which are utilised in philosophical argument.

A panchreston is a word which appears to have a precise meaning when it does not, but it is used as if it did, to further a logical argument. The fallacy is to accredit the word a meaning for the sake of argument, but to forget this has been done and to go on supposing that the word does represent concrete reality.

Szasz suggests that schizophrenia is just such a panchreston. It was a useful concept invented to aid our thinking about certain types of behaviour, but we have fallen into the error of thinking that beyond this it has a concrete reality. Like the Sorcerer's Apprentice, we have become the victims of our own thinking. But not everyone would agree with Szasz, and many workers believe that schizophrenia exists as a single entity or at least as a group of entities which have a definite existence of their own, and do not merely mirror aspects of our own thinking. Such workers try to distinguish between nuclear or *process schizophrenias*, which are believed to form a basic group due to active pathological disease processes, and *symptomatic schizophrenias*, which are illnesses like schizophrenia but are released in susceptible persons by other concurrent illnesses such as brain tumour, brain injury or infection.

A further group of disorders are called the *schizophreniform psychoses*, which are schizophrenia-like but are due to a variety of causes, including pure psychological states (psychogenic psychoses), and have a quite different prognosis or outcome. True schizophrenia or process schizophrenia, following the view of Kraepelin, is held to be a relapsing and progressive disorder.

Definitions

Schizophrenia remains a chimera, a will-o'-the-wisp, that eludes its pursuers and refuses to be pinned down. We can all recognise schizophrenic patients, that is those who behave in a certain way and show all the symptoms which we associate with the schizophrenic process, but when we try to set down precisely what schizophrenia is, the definition is rarely fully satisfactory. This has led people to ask if schizophrenia exists at all as a psychiatric entity, and suggests that all we can define are certain patterns of behaviour in our patients which have a schizophrenic quality. In other words, schizophrenia does not exist as such, but patients can show schizophrenic behaviour.

Thus we should always use it in an adjective rather than in a nominal form. In a way this applies to all illnesses which affect human beings. We talk loosely of 'tuberculosis', but the illness can never exist in its own right; it can only manifest itself by the interaction of an affecting agent with a susceptible host. Thus we should not really talk of defining schizophrenia, but of defining the ways in which provoking factors can interact with predisposed individuals to produce the behaviour patterns which we call, for convenience, schizophrenia.

Others will not accept this viewpoint and still seek to define schizophrenia as an illness, according to different parameters:

(*a*) By *nosology*: that is, by its place in the classification of psychiatric disorders. Nosology states that schizophrenia is a psychotic disorder, a major psychiatric illness, and that it belongs to the subgroup of the functional psychoses.

(*b*) By *clinical description*: that is, by how it is experienced in clinical practice. Schizophrenia is a group of serious mental disorders characterised by disorder of thought, feeling and perception which leads to a disruption of will and of organised behaviour.

(*c*) By *supposed aetiology*: that is, by the various beliefs as to how the disorder comes about. Schizophrenia is a group of serious mental disorders caused by disease of the brain, or by specific forms of acute anxiety, or by an acute breakdown of personality structure, etc.

It is this impreciseness of definition and the difficulty of arriving at accepted criteria of diagnosis that give rise to most of the present-day controversy about the exact nature, causes and management of schizophrenia.

Current views

These differ widely on a world-wide basis, and reflect the various schools of psychiatry uppermost at the time, as well as the impreciseness of definition already discussed.

The *European view*, with its long tradition founded in the schools of anatomy and pathology, emphasises the organic explanation which seeks to find the causes of the disorder in disease of the brain or in disturbances of the brain metabolism.

This view regards schizophrenia as an illness best conceived on the well-tried and traditional model of physical illness. Research is concentrated on the examination of the brain function at a macroscopic or microscopic level using the techniques of histology, physiology, pharmacology, neuropathology and biochemistry.

The *American view*, with its long tradition founded in the

Psychoanalytic and the Psychobiological Schools, sees schizophrenia as a behavioural disorder due to a variety of causes of a psychological and social nature, such as unresolved oedipal conflicts or particular patterns of family relationships. Research is centred on the examination of the breakdown of mental mechanisms which normally deal with primitive anxiety, and of disturbed patterns of interpersonal communication.

The *British view* comes somewhere between these extremes, in a compromise position which holds that the central or nuclear group of schizophrenias is primarily due to organic processes yet to be convincingly demonstrated, and that the more peripheral group of schizophrenias are of varied but uncertain origins, but including psychological and interpersonal causes.

These are necessarily extreme expressions of the three views, but represent the most commonly held position of the major world areas involved in research. In any one country, all three views may be represented, but one tends to be the dominant one. Each of these views will be discussed in detail at the end of this part, after the clinical presentation and personal experience of schizophrenic patients have been described.

Clinical Features

(a) Incidence and prevalence

Incidence measures the number of new cases arising each year in a given population, and is a measure of expectancy within that population. Despite the difficulty in precise definition of the disorder, and the widespread views of its nature, there is a surprising degree of agreement in all workers as to the expectancy of schizophrenia in different kinds of populations. This expectancy rate in the general population is 0.85 per cent or just under 1 in every 100.

Prevalence measures the number of cases of any given condition in a population at a given time, and is a measure of the burden on the caring facilities.

In this country about 50 per cent of all hospital beds in the National Health Service are in psychiatric hospitals, and about 50 per cent of these psychiatric beds are occupied by schizophrenic patients. It has been estimated that approximately 60 000 schizophrenics are being treated on an in-patient basis in the psychiatric hospitals in England and Wales.

But how many schizophrenics are out in the community? From an estimate of expectancy in the population age groups at risk in England and Wales it can be said that for every one schizophrenic in a hospital bed there are probably four or five out in the community. Many of these, however, are being treated on an out-patient basis or are attending day centres, but nevertheless it probably means that there are a number of schizophrenics unrecognised as such and living in the community. Many of them are classified as eccentric or 'odd' people, while others occupy a prison cell or travel the roads of this country as vagrants.

As a measure of expectancy it has been said that 1 man in 14 and 1 woman in 9 spend some time during their lives in a psychiatric hospital, and that 1 family in 5 will have a member destined to have psychiatric treatment in a psychiatric hospital.

This does not mean that they will necessarily suffer from a schizophrenic disorder, but the chance remains quite high.

The issue of expectancy becomes crucial in *genetic counselling* when a family wishes to know what are the chances of a member of that family having a schizophrenic disorder when there is perhaps a history of a distant relative having been treated for this disorder in a hospital. Research has given us a number of useful indications of approximate risk:

The risk in the general population equals 0·8 per cent or 1 in 125. If one child is schizophrenic, the risk for a blood brother or sister equals 14 per cent or 1 in 7.

If one parent is schizophrenic, the risk to the children of the union equals 14 per cent or 1 in 7.

If both parents are schizophrenic, the risk to the children of the union equals 40 per cent or 1 in 2·5.

If a twin is schizophrenic, the risk for a non-identical twin is the same as for ordinary brothers and sisters, namely 14 per cent, but if the twins are identical the risk rises to well over 50 per cent—authorities remain divided as to how high the actual risk is.

These can be broad guidelines only. In any particular case the full family history on both sides of the union have to be taken into account, and a balance sheet drawn up as it were of both the good and the bad points.

b) Symptoms

These are what patients complain of. The symptoms are his own personal way of experiencing his disorder and are what he reports to his doctor. Each schizophrenic patient experiences his disorder in his own individual way, which makes each patient unique and different from all other patients, but there are a number of symptoms which are very common and shared by all or most schizophrenics.

They come and say that they are *confused and perplexed*: something is happening to them that they do not understand. They experience *disturbing inner feelings*: often they say that they are dead, or that they have been changed in some way, often that they are changing sex or have been changed into someone else or even into an animal; they feel that they are being stimulated and they talk of being electrified or of being influenced by wireless waves or radar beams playing on them from outer space.

As a result of these experiences, many claim to be *persecuted*: they can only make sense of these inner disturbances by supposing they are due to some hostile external force. For most there is a feeling of *growing isolation* as they themselves or the world around them change in these upsetting ways; they find they cannot communicate with other people and cannot judge other people's reactions to themselves; they feel shut off and alienated. They even *perceive the world in a different way*; people around them look different or sound different or behave in unexpected ways. All this releases inside them feelings of anxiety, fear, panic and even terror. They feel they are *losing control* over their own actions and over those of the people around them. They fear being *overwhelmed* as they experience a gradual loss of *personal identity*.

A British psychiatrist, Dr R. D. Laing, has described in two books—*The Divided Self* and *The Self and Others*—this personal experience of inner and outer disintegration as the schizophrenic process develops inside patients. They feel that external reality is growing too much for them and that they are going to be engulfed by it, or else feel such a loss of personal identity that they do not know when they themselves and others begin so that they fear being absorbed into others or that others will be absorbed into them.

It is because of this experience that schizophrenics feel that they are to blame for all the evil in the world; they feel that they are personally to blame for major disasters because the evil that is inside them has leaked out and poisoned the world. It is easy to see how in medieval times such persons could by their own testimony be accused of witchcraft or sorcery.

The experiences of schizophrenics, although confusing and disturbing, can be made sense of if we can keep clear two separate processes. First, there is the basic alteration of experience due to the schizophrenic disorder; second, there is the attempt of the schizophrenic patient to make sense of what is happening.

For example, a patient may report that he is being persecuted by hidden aggressors, and that as a result his thoughts and feelings are being taken out of his body. This patient primarily feels changed in his awareness of himself and then secondarily tries to explain why this is happening by the mechanism of paranoid projection, that is putting the blame on someone else. This person cannot be clearly identified, so he remains present but hidden all the time. Because he feels differently, he supposes it must be because something has been taken away from him by the hidden persecutor. Because the patient is, from the standpoint of the observer, mistaken in his interpretation and explanation of what is happening, some classify schizophrenia as a misinterpretative state.

There is also a dispute concerning the exact nature of what is happening to the patient. Traditional workers see the patient's symptoms as evidence of the disease process itself, while others, like R. D. Laing, seek to understand the symptoms as being the person's attempt to find his true self again. In the first view, symptoms are to be suppressed and treated, but in the second view the same symptoms are to be encouraged and supported. The dispute is similar to that about fever. Fever was thought originally to be a disease itself, but research has shown that the raised temperature is one way by which the body defends itself against external infection. Both views are tenable and need not be mutually exclusive.

Patients' symptoms can be both the evidence of a disorder and at the same time a token of the attempt by the personality to deal with that disorder.

(c) Clinical signs

These are the disturbances of function which the trained observer notes and which are taken with the symptoms to establish the diagnosis. The symptoms are what the patient experiences, and the signs are what is observed and experienced by others. Schizophrenia as a mental disorder affects all aspects of psychic life and leads to a disruption and division of them. The normal integration and co-ordination of psychic function is disjointed and the mind becomes divided in and against itself. The disorder affects thinking, feeling, perceiving, willing and behaving.

1 Thinking

Thinking is the basic activity of the mind. In schizophrenia thinking is typically vague and woolly because the internal coherence has gone. What Bleuler called the central determining theme, which in others gives a direction and flow to normal thought, is missing and as a result the patient loses control over his thought processes. His speech, which reflects his thought, is rambling and at times can be incoherent. Such structure that there is, is often fortuitous and based on strange associations—'I feel my life is death, because of the death of feeling which arises out of the earth, which is me but empty, poor empty me, pity me for God's sake; is this goodness which I lack? Good God, has it come to this?'

His speech is full of puns, and rhyming association. He also tends to become preoccupied with introspection, philosophy and obscure religious ideas. As he feels his control over his thinking and speech going, he tries to find answers to the changes in himself and the changes in the world around him. He may ask questions like 'What is me?' 'Who am I?' 'What is being?' but rarely in a constructive or helpful context. He tries to find language to express changes in consciousness of himself and others, and makes up new words (neologisms) to describe these new experiences.

As the dissolution of coherent thinking advances the patient shows evidence of what is called formal thought disorder. A number of common features are seen. There is *thought blocking* in which the flow of thought suddenly ceases and then after a gap starts again but on a different theme. 'I feel the world is pressing down on top of me; I feel frightened —what day is it today?—why are you wearing blue?' The experience of a new train of thought is often felt as *thought insertion* as if new thoughts were being put into his mind from an outside source. The actual block is experienced as *thought withdrawal*—thoughts literally taken out of his mind. Using the simile of the train of thought, the rapid shifts from one topic to another and the disruption are described as *thought derailment.*

Many people wonder about the existence of extra sensory perception (ESP), that process whereby it is believed one person can read the unspoken thoughts of another at a distance. ESP still remains to be proven scientifically, but many people relate circumstances in which another has happened to 'know' what is going on in their mind. Schizophrenics have this feeling very strongly and it probably is based on the assumption that if others can interrupt one's thoughts and insert other thoughts into one's mind, then it is logical that they can know one's thoughts as well. This experience is known as *thought broadcasting*—the idea that one's own private thoughts are no longer one's own, but are picked up by others around one.

Schizophrenics have another experience which they describe in various ways. Each of us is aware of our own thoughts inside our heads. We can appreciate them at a sub-vocal level; we do not have to articulate the thoughts in order to know what we think. This is the same process as 'silent reading'. We can if we wish make our thoughts come aloud inside our heads, but they still remain sub-vocal. We appreciate them 'as if' they were heard aloud, but we do not experience them as actual voices.

The schizophrenic, on the other hand, will often say that he hears his own thoughts aloud inside his head. This is called in German *Gedankenlautverden*—his thoughts appear to be spoken aloud by a voice, which often is experienced as different from his own, and can be recognised as being male or female. Not only are his thoughts heard aloud, but the voice appears to keep up a running commentary on what he is doing. 'Now he is going to look over there; now he is going to open the door.' This gives the schizophrenic the further impression that he is a passive object under the observation and control of others around him.

The thoughts of schizophrenics are often delusional. A *delusion* is a false belief, out of keeping with the cultural context of the patient and which is unshakable. These delusions can either be grandiose—a belief that he is someone greater than he really is—the origin of those stories of schizophrenics calling themselves Julius Caesar or Napoleon or Queen of the Universe; or they can be paranoid—a belief that he is being persecuted by others, often on the premise that others recognise his delusional greatness and are jealous of it; or they can be delusions of poverty—a conviction that he has lost all his money, lost all position in the family, that he is a nothing, a veritable shadow of his former self.

There is a special group of delusional experiences called *autochthonous delusions* which are said to be diagnostic of schizophrenia (delusions do occur in psychotic conditions other than schizophrenic ones). Here the schizophrenic just knows that something is; for example, he might say that he is convinced that he is to be killed because the trees shake in the wind. This is an unshakable belief in which there is no logical connection between his observation and his conclusions. These autochthonous delusions are believed to arise out of what again in German is called *Wahnstimmung* or delusional mood. The primary disorder is an altered feeling which is then misinterpreted in a delusional way.

2 Feeling

Feeling is an emotional experience in response to the world around us. Schizophrenics have what are called *passivity feelings*; that is, the belief that they are no longer in charge of themselves but passively are influenced by forces around them. It is easy to see how such a belief arises out of the experience that one's private thoughts are no longer one's own but are interfered with and altered by outside forces. In order to feel that we are in charge of ourselves, we have to have a sense of identity and purpose, and a conviction that we are free to respond to our circumstances as we choose. It is this very freedom that the schizophrenic lacks.

In addition, the schizophrenic's feelings are said to be *blunted, flattened* and *stilted*. These words are used to describe the quality of lacking freshness, spontaneity and variety. The range of emotional responses with which schizophrenics react to life situations is reduced, and the affect or mood is one of emptiness or one of automatic, almost programmed, nature. As well as being altered in quantity the emotional response shown by schizophrenics is often incongruous, and we speak of *incongruity of affect* by which is meant that the feelings shown are out of context and inappropriate to the circumstances. For example, the patient may appear to be hilariously happy when a mood of quietness or even unhappiness would be expected. Perhaps it is because a schizophrenic is so unsure of himself that he cannot judge how others around him are feeling; in other words, he has a defective emotional feedback. This would certainly result in a misjudging of the mood of the group and lead to behaviour and feeling out of keeping with that of the others.

The flattening of affect and its incongruity is what is

experienced by others as a very characteristic brick-wall effect called *lack of rapport.* In relationship with others, we quickly sense a mutual exchange of congruous feelings. We feel at one with the other; a sense of being with him which is called rapport. If we cannot establish rapport with another we quickly lose interest in him and go off in search of someone else with whom this emotional link can be established. Rapport is based on a mutual recognition and reciprocation of the feeling state of the other. This the schizophrenic is unable to achieve with us, and unless we are prepared to be very patient and tolerant we cannot achieve it with him. To most people, this brick-wall effect of being unable to make meaningful contact is too anxiety provoking, and they quickly move away and avoid the schizophrenic. This in turn can reinforce any tendency to paranoia which he may have.

3 Perceiving

Perceiving is the process whereby we register what is going on around us, and make sense of it by relating it to past experience. Our external and internal worlds are relayed to us by means of the five senses: seeing, hearing, tasting, smelling and touching. A sensory stimulus releases a perceptive response. For example, we 'see' a person approaching us and recognise that he is a friend. We can, however, make mistakes; we see someone coming, we believe he is a friend we know, but as he comes nearer we see that we are mistaken. He is only like our friend. Likewise, we can mistake a shadow moving in a dimly lit room for an actual animal. Our senses have been deceived. This experience is called an *illusion*: we mistake an actual stimulus. Occasionally we can have a sensory experience when there is no preceding stimulus, and this is called an *hallucination*. When we are fevered or toxic we may have what are like waking dreams: we see and hear people around us who are not there. In some toxic states we can be pursued by hallucinatory predators—the famous pink elephants of the inebriate. This can happen to all of us, but schizophrenics experience illusions and hallucinations more often. Commonly, these are in the form of voices which are different from the spoken thoughts already described. The spoken thoughts are heard inside the patient's head, but the hallucinatory voices are usually heard outside the patient and are given a separate existence. These voices are often critical and distressing, and may provoke the patient into impulsive actions to escape from them. Less commonly, the hallucinations are visual, the patient experiencing a vision often of religious content. Joan of Arc had her visions and her voices that talked to her. These may have been of schizophrenic origin, but on the other hand hallucinations and mystical experiences occur to others who are not necessarily schizophrenic.

In other patients, the hallucinations are somatised; that is, they are felt as bodily sensations which underly the common belief that the patient is changing sex, being interfered with sexually in some way by external agencies, or the frequent complaint that they are being electrified or being influenced by wireless waves or radar beams.

Hallucinations are commonly found in schizophrenia, but they do occur in many other states, not all of which are necessarily abnormal, but they are such unusual and odd human experiences that if we have them we do not like to tell others about them, lest they think that we are going mad.

4 Willing

Willing is the process whereby we determine what we want to be and what we want to do. It is also the process by which we find the energy and drive to put these ambitions into effect. The motivation behind our willpower is either a positive drive to achieve, and thereby to be rewarded, or a negative drive to avoid unpleasant situations and pain. This, however, presupposes that we can think clearly, appreciate the feelings of ourselves and others, and perceive accurately the world in which we find ourselves.

It is hardly surprising, then, to find that the schizophrenic who is disturbed in his thinking, feeling and perceiving is also disturbed in his willing. Most patients lack drive and ambition, and gradually sink down into a life of social incompetence. Others have episodic but sustained outbursts of drive in which they pursue haphazardly the impulse of the moment. Neither pattern leads to efficient living and that is why so many schizophrenics drift into vagrancy, into unskilled employment and into the poorer part of large cities. The schizophrenic living in rural areas can appear to be less incompetent and survive longer in the community, but that is only because he is not exposed to so many or so varied demands upon him.

5 *Behaving*

Behaving is the final outcome of thinking, feeling, perceiving and willing. If all these are disturbed, behaviour must be disturbed as well. It is odd behaviour which often first brings the schizophrenic to notice—the things he says, his unusual beliefs, the complicated rituals by which he protects himself from a hostile world. Often he will neglect himself—not eat or wash, nor take elementary precautions over illness. He may look for an easy way out through alcohol or drugs. If he is paranoid and his voices goad him on, he may attack those whom he believes to be his persecutors. If all else fails, he may attack himself, turning his hopeless fury and despair inwards in an irrational act of self-mutilation or of self-destruction.

When the world is a frightening place in which you feel yourself becoming more isolated and out of contact, complicated rituals are devised to ward off evil influences—hoarding objects which have magical power in the form of charms or amulets, performing repetitive acts, cutting down the chance of being caught out by surrounding oneself with a miniature world controlled by an obsessional defence.

For the schizophrenic the smallest object may be the source of greatest danger—the crack in the floor, the hole in the wall, the speck of dirt in the food; complicated daily routines have to be devised whereby the hidden dangers can be avoided. Anything unpredictable is particularly dangerous, and so the schizophrenic becomes a creature of habit with his own idiosyncratic mannerisms and repetitive behaviours known as stereotypes. Many of his actions have a symbolic and magical significance, all designed to protect his disintegrating self from the encroachments of a hostile environment.

The Schizophrenic's World

Being a schizophrenic is not quite the same as suffering from other disorders, psychological or physical. Having a broken leg or suffering from an infection or a chronic disability like arthritis does not involve the personality of the sufferer to such a major degree. The inner life of the person, although influenced by the disorder from which he suffers, is not threatened in quite the same way. The life of the person who is the patient can continue much as it did before he developed the disorder from which he is now suffering. He may have to curtail his activities to a degree; he may have to go to bed, give up his job or realise that what he could do before will in the future not be so easy or so possible, but his perception of himself as a person and the social setting in which he expresses that personality are not changed to a radical degree.

His concept of himself may be diminished, but it is not utterly changed. He is still himself in historical continuity with the self before the illness, and the self to come after the illness. But in schizophrenia that is not so, because there is a break in the continuity of self and the whole concept of self may be under attack and threatened in a very basic way.

To become schizophrenic is to become a new person in a new world. Experience changes not only in degree but also in quality. All values and presuppositions are no longer there to rely on and by which to orientate oneself. The cardinal points of the compass have been changed and the needle swings under the influence of new kinds of forces.

Some argue that this change is a retrogressive one, and that the individual is retreating into a more primitive, infantile style of life; others argue that this change opens up possibilities for new growth and development which had been stifled before, by the very ordinariness and ordering of everyday life. They hold that the tedium of living in a world of conformity and to the will of the establishment blurs the vision of what we once might have become, and that the schizophrenic disorder breaks up the habitual patterns of thinking and feeling and perceiving, and allows the personality to escape into a newness of life.

This is a minority view: for the majority of patients, the schizophrenic experience is a terrifying and destructive one which leads to progressive deterioration and poverty of living which is acted out against the background of medical care, much of it in the setting of the psychiatric hospital.

We who are not schizophrenic can enter a little into the subjective world of the schizophrenic through the glimpses which he gives of himself—his reactions, his relationships, his perceptions as he reveals them in artistic creations—in drawings, paintings, sculpture, poems and in the inner world of experience which he reveals in his responses to psychological tests.

(a) Art of the schizophrenic

We have to distinguish at the beginning between artistic creations which seem to us to be strange and mystical, and which appear to reflect the world of madness but are the works of normal artists, and those often childlike in technique which are the work of genuinely disturbed schizophrenic persons. The first can only guess at what madness feels like, but the second can show it to us in all its terror and perplexity.

When schizophrenics write narrative accounts of what it is like to be them, there is a dilemma. When they are acutely disturbed and the experience is at its height, ordinary words lose their power to describe what is happening. New words (neologisms) and new ways of self-expression have to be employed which then are meaningless to those who read them afterwards. But when a schizophrenic writes in a state of remission, communication with us is easier, but he himself may have lost sight of the essential quality of the schizophrenic process when it was at its height.

Poetry lends itself to more symbolic and condensed communication, using verbal imagery. Here we have reflections of the loneliness, the isolation, the perplexity and despair of being mad:

> 'The confines of the mind are loosed
> And clouds confuse the inner eye.
> When shall we know that powerful light
> That shows us truth and certainty?'

and as William Blake has said:

> '—Thought is life
> And strength and breath,
> And the want
> Of thought is death.'

It appears easier to convey chaotic ideas and disturbing feelings in images rather than words. The ordinary schizophrenic of average intelligence finds it easier to draw and to paint than to write of his inner experience. This may only indicate that images are more direct, more immediate than words in their impact (one good picture is worth a thousand words); also images are more concise; with words we can invest them with our own fantasies, but images declare openly and directly the fantasy which the artist wishes to share with us.

Why do schizophrenics produce pictures at all? It would seem obvious as a means of communication, but communication with whom? The artist is producing something for an audience, but in a very real sense he is producing something for himself. He is communicating with himself and we are looking over his shoulder. This is an ancient function of art which enters the realm of magic.

Primitive man painted wild creatures on the walls of his cave not just for decoration but for a purpose. He felt that if he could capture the animal in its likeness on the wall, he would be able to capture it in the field. Giving something a name and a shape and enclosing it within a symbol gave the creator power over the object whose image he had created. Likewise, it would appear that the schizophrenic regains a sense of control over things if he can put down on paper images and symbols of the chaotic world in which he finds himself.

This would explain why many patients find an artistic interest and talent released in them during a psychotic episode, which then disappears when they return to normal again. This period of creativity is functional in a very primitive sense; it is a means of mastery over the illusive environment. Another explanation is that these same symbols and images arise out of the dark unconscious part of the mind. Normally, these are held in check by what is called the Censor, and can only escape in modified form in dreams, but the psychotic process involves a weakening of the boundaries of the unconscious and the conscious, and these images and symbols well up into the conscious mind demanding to be expressed.

The content of schizophrenic art shows a preoccupation with the occult, with magic, miracle and myth. In our every-day lives we are preoccupied with what we choose to call the real world, and if we are dimly aware of the world of shadows and mystery we choose to ignore it as we pursue the pragmatic and the concrete. But for the schizophrenic things have become reversed—the real world of ours is for him the world of shadows, and he is deeply preoccupied with the world of inner exploration. For him the subjective has become objective, and the shadows have taken on substance and form.

It is this directness with the indirect which gives a literalism to schizophrenic painting, which it shares with primitive art. Sympathetic magic expresses itself in two ways: in an imitative form in which representation of the object gives us power over it, and in a contagious form in which representation of the object allows us to inherit the power of the object. Painting a bison on the cave wall gave the paleolithic artist power to capture the bison in the hunt, but it also gave him, he believed, the qualities of the bison which he coveted—power, strength and courage.

We can see in schizophrenics' pictures, if we analyse them carefully, a reflection of the psychotic process and the psychotic experience. We can see the repetition of the signs and symptoms we have already described. There is an absence of depth—the figures have no volume or bodiliness; there are no shadows to be cast because of the objects' insubstantiality. There is an absence of substance —line takes precedence over texture, which, if it is there, is only crudely represented. Anatomy is simplified, distorted and symbolised. There is an absence of movement—figures are static, captured in the second of time which is endless. The outlines are prominent, defined often by single stroke and rapid execution. Shapes are geometric with stylised hatching. Form is condensed with a transparent view. Style is dehumanised, ornamental and abstract. All these reflect the emptiness, flatness, uncertainty and doubt which the person feels, and an attempt to capture in a precise and defined way what to him is illusive and illusionary.

There are a number of recurring subjects seen in schizophrenic pictures. What are called composite figures remind us of modern artists who display two dimensions equally in the same plane; we may see front and side and even back juxtaposed in the style of Piccasso. There are cephalopods—compressed figures whose heads are immediately joined to the feet with little or no body between. There are transparent or

'X-ray men' through which we can see what lies behind. And over and over again there is the symbol of the eye. This may be a complex visual pun:

$$eye = I \ (me) = Ego = existence$$

The eye which is portrayed may represent the 'watching eye': the ever-controlling presence from which the schizophrenic is trying to escape. It may be the 'all-seeing eye' from which there is truly no escape and which sees deep into the heart of our being. It may be the 'eye of power', the sacred eye painted on the prow of vessels to steer the ship to its chosen harbour, or the 'evil eye' through which another can gain power and control over us for his own purpose. It may be the 'eye of the artist' looking at us as we in turn look at him through the medium of what he has put down on paper.

In all this, we can become too introspective and certainty can be replaced with guesswork. We can only truly know what the schizophrenic means if we ask him, but here there is a difficulty, for these very paintings have been chosen to be a way of expressing the inexpressible. Discussing his paintings with a patient and correlating this with his symptoms and what he can tell us about himself in other circumstances gives us an idea of what it is like to be him. But it remains as an idea only. We can only look into madness 'as if into a glass darkly'.

(b) In psychology

In art the schizophrenic makes his creation out of basic raw materials which he moulds and shapes from his imagination to express what he feels about his world of experience. The clinical psychologist, who works with the psychiatrist in trying to understand and help the schizophrenic, presents him with ready-made situations and then analyses what he does with them.

These ready-made situations can be questions to which specific answers are expected, or they can be complex visual patterns to be completed; they can be picture stories to arrange or unstructured stimuli like ink blots to be interpreted, designed to liberate free association. The responses to these set situations can then be compared from one individual to another, between groups of persons, and between schizophrenic patients and those who are not schizophrenic. The psychologist is therefore not only analysing the details of the performance of the individual being tested, but also comparing his performance to that of others who have gone before, and who are believed to belong to the same diagnostic group. Psychological tests can be used in two ways: firstly, as a diagnostic instrument to complement the clinical assessment made by the psychiatrist and, secondly, to gain insight into how the schizophrenic thinks, feels, perceives and interprets his environment, which in this instance is the tester and the test material which he sets before the patient. Thus the psychologist provides another gateway through which we can again glimpse something of the world of the schizophrenic—how he feels about himself and about the objects and people around him.

Psychological Tests

H. Y. Robertson, MA
Clinical Psychologist, Fulbourn Hospital, Cambridge

The psychiatric patient in hospital comes into contact with many different people—psychiatrists, nurses, social workers, occupational therapists and others. One person he may be asked to see is the clinical psychologist. The psychologist has various functions, including teaching psychology to others, carrying out research into mental illness, and therapy. But he is probably best known through the psychological tests he uses, and which sometimes prompt the response from a patient who has seen him—'That was a waste of time. All he did was show me a lot of silly ink blots.'

Psychological tests are used with most types of psychiatric patients, but they are of particular value with the schizophrenic. In this illness, different areas of an individual's functioning may be affected, causing him to view his world differently from when he is well. The psychologist, by using refined tests, can help to elicit a clearer picture of the schizophrenic's world.

The value of the tests used by the psychologist is perhaps best illustrated by an actual case study. The patient was a research worker, a young man in his twenties, admitted to hospital suffering from an acute paranoid schizophrenic illness. The most obvious symptom of his illness was that he thought an international gang was trying to kill him. He was referred to the psychologist to determine whether this was an isolated

lelusion or whether it encroached on other aspects of
his life.

Conversation with him was very easy. In fact, apart from
his specific delusion, there was little to indicate why he should
have been in hospital. Because of his seemingly 'normal'
manner, he was not considered to be thought disordered. A
battery of tests covering intellectual and personality areas was
administered, to give as wide ranging a picture as possible.
It was soon obvious that his illness was more extensive than
had at first been thought.

His score on the Wechsler Adult Intelligence Scale (WAIS),
the most widely used intelligence test, was around the average
for the general population. In his case this was highly significant because as a research worker he should have scored
considerably higher. By analysing his response to individual
items within the test, it was conclusively demonstrated how
thought-disordered he actually was. His thinking was highly
idiosyncratic (personalised) and showed evidence both of
'blocking', where he appeared to stop dead in the train of a
thought, and 'concreteness', where he was unable to think in
the abstract terms expected of someone in his line of work.
These disorders of thinking were confirmed by tests specially
designed to elicit the presence of this type of disfunction.

The two personality tests which he did were both 'projective' tests, and it is these which tend to provoke the sort of
response quoted earlier. One, the Rorschach Test, consists of
a series of ink blots, the patient being required to say what
they remind him of or look like. Why ask patients to look at
ink blots at all? It has been found that people suffering from
different illnesses give different kinds of responses to the unstructured stimuli, and the psychologist by analysing them
can give help in those cases where diagnosis is difficult, and
also provide information which will be useful in the general
management of the patient. However, it must not be assumed
that such tests come up with a complete answer every time, as
few cases are so clear cut. In this particular example, the
patient's mode of perceiving these ambiguous stimuli indi-

cated the presence of a considerable depressive element, as well as a paranoia.

The other projective test which he did was the Thematic Apperception Test, popularly known as the TAT. Here the patient is presented with pictures showing people in a variety of situations, and he has to make up stories about them. The stories give an insight into his inner mental life, indicating what conflicts and anxieties he has, how he interacts with other people, how he interprets what he perceives in the 'normal' environment. Information about his parental relationships and his difficulties in heterosexual relationships (relationships with members of the opposite sex) was obtained, which was relevant to his subsequent treatment.

The case study shows that the psychologist's equipment contains more than just ink blots, but that when he asks the schizophrenic or any other patient to perform the task of looking at these blots, the psychologist is doing something other than just trying to mystify the patient. He is attempting to gather a body of information which will provide an objective picture of the illness, and pointers for treatment and rehabilitation. The clinical psychologist is another member of the team whose aim is to return the schizophrenic to the life in the community with which he is most able to cope.

Classifying the Schizophrenias

We have spoken so far as if schizophrenia were a unitary concept, but as Bleuler pointed out in his original monograph in 1911, the schizophrenias are a group of disorders having a number of features in common which we have been examining up to now. Classification is a means whereby different patterns of behaviour can be put into descriptive categories so that we can understand more clearly the differences as well as the similarities between them. These differences are very important because it is exactly the ways in which conditions differ that suggest possible causes and therefore possible management. The descriptive categories used are as follows:

(a) **Typology:** that is, classification by the clinical features shown by the patient

Hebephrenic schizophrenia: occurs in younger patients, females more than males, and is characterised by disturbance of thinking, feeling, perceiving, willing and behaving. The young person is giggly and fatuous, often markedly deluded and behaves in a very 'mad' way. Ophelia in Hamlet is a good example, and, like Ophelia, the hebephrenic can become so disturbed that in the end she may destroy herself.

Paranoid schizophrenia: occurs in older patients, males more than females, and is characterised by disturbance of thinking, feeling and behaving. The patient is deluded, believing himself to be the object of persecution, and acts accordingly to defend himself. He is usually passionate in the intensity with which he will defend the validity of his delusions. He is rarely hallucinated and may appear quite normal until someone touches upon a sensitive subject which releases all his paranoia. The paranoid form also occurs in much older patients, in the senile age group, and here females are more often affected than males and they may be actively hallucinated as well.

Catatonic schizophrenia is less commonly seen nowadays, but the disorder is characterised by disturbance of thinking, feeling and behaving. The patient behaves in unusual ways, becoming more and more slowed up until he may come to a stuporose standstill in which he will remain in stylised postures for long periods of time. He will not respond to questioning then, but may recall later all that went on, much to the consternation of anyone who thought that he was 'unconscious' and not aware of what was being said about him. In classic cases, the patient's muscles showed what was called 'waxy flexibility' whereby his limbs could be bent into grotesque postures and held there as if the muscles were made of pliant wax. The catatonic was also liable to impulsive outbursts of aggression, often as the result of being beleaguered by hallucinatory voices.

Simple schizophrenia is the least easy to diagnose. These patients do not show obviously disordered thinking, but are flattened in their feelings, lacking in ambition and drift down the social scale. They are difficult to distinguish from eccentrics who become vagrants or those very inadequate persons who cannot cope with life's problems and drift into a life of social disorganisation as a result.

It must be emphasised that these types are not clearly differentiated but blend one into the other. The types described represent the most extreme examples.

b) Aetiology: that is, classification by supposed causation

Primary schizophrenias: believed to be due to a specific centrally acting pathological process. These are described as the central, nuclear or process schizophrenias.

Secondary schizophrenias: believed to be released by some other non-specific co-incident disorder; for example, brain injury, toxic state or childbirth. These are described as the released or symptomatic schizophrenias.

(c) Phasing: that is, classification by the time of development of the disorder

Acute onset schizophrenias: these are the rapidly developing disorders which arise out of a non-psychotic state. The disorder as a group is believed, as Bleuler said, to have a variable course, characterised by acute episodes, with relapses and remissions leading to a chronic end state.

Chronic schizophrenias: these are the end states of the acute forms, and the patient remains in a state of perpetual psychosis in which he rarely if ever returns to any degree of his previous pre-morbid level of function.

(d) Prognosis: that is, classification by probable outcome

The true schizophrenias: believed to have the classical variable course ending in the inevitable chronic breakdown of personality and of psychic life.

The schizophreniform reactions: these are psychotic episodes indistinguishable except in the finest detail from the classical schizophrenias, but in which an acute attack may not lead on to a chronically progressive course but may be aborted never to return again, or, if it does, to show a complete remission after each relapse.

(e) Age groups: that is, classification by the time of life in which the disorder manifests itself.

Childhood schizophrenias: these cases are exceedingly rare, and have to be distinguished from another group of severely disturbed children classified as suffering from infantile autism.

Adolescent schizophrenias: these are the most commonly occurring group, usually first appearing about the age of fourteen or fifteen years, and the full disorder being established by about nineteen or twenty years.

Puerperal schizophrenias: a special group which appears in the period immediately following on the birth of a child, and which is associated with the dangers of infant neglect or infanticide.

Late onset schizophrenias: these come on in middle adult life and may be associated with a sensory defect, such as blindness or deafness, or in situations of extreme social isolation.

Senile schizophrenias: these are the rare group of disorders which come on for the first time as old age advances and are associated with confusion and evidence of other organic changes in the brain.

The importance of such classifications is not only to make sense out of an otherwise confusing motley of disorders, but also to suggest possible differences in causation, outcome and management.

Predicting the Outcome

For the patient it may be more important to know the outcome or prognosis of his disorder than it is to know its nature or diagnosis. There are a number of questions he will want to ask.

'Will I have to go into hospital for treatment?' 'Will I get better?' 'How long will it take?' 'When I am better, will I have any residual disability?' 'Will this disorder ever come back again?' 'Will this disorder affect any of my children?' 'Will I be able to go back to my old job?' 'Will I be able to drive my car?' 'Will I be able to adopt a child?' 'Will I be able to get a visa to emigrate?' 'Will it affect my ability to conduct my own affairs?'

All those questions and many others like them reflect the anxiety of the patient about his personal integrity. Will the disorder destroy his personality? If he recovers, how full will the recovery be? Will he be diminished in any way as a human being as a result of this disorder? Does it only affect him or will it also affect those who are dependent upon him? What are his chances?

Prognosis remains one of the arts of medicine. Attempts have been made to quantify a risk on an actuarial basis, that is by weighing all the factors present to determine a precise percentage risk and to place the risk for the given patient in the perspective of accumulated data about similar patients. Such attempts have been limited by the same impreciseness of definition and diagnosis which we have noted previously. Prognosis remains an art which can only be learned by hard experience. The doctor who has looked after many schizophrenic patients begins to 'know' those who will be likely to do well and those who will not. This 'knowing' is based upon a number of guiding observations.

The outlook is better with:

(*a*) A later age of onset of the clinical features.

(*b*) An acute onset and stormy development of the disorder.

(*c*) An obvious precipitating cause.

(*d*) A large emotionally active component.

(*e*) An absent family history of mental disorder.

(*f*) A pyknic habitus, that is bulky body build.

(*g*) A previously good well-integrated personality.

(*h*) Intelligence in the mid range, neither too low nor too high.

(*i*) A demonstrable metabolic or organic cause.

(*j*) A hebephrenic or catatonic type rather than a paranoid or simple type.

It can be seen that generally the more acute the onset of the illness and the more disturbed the patient is, the better is the outcome, but if the disorder comes on slowly and insidiously and the patient's disorder does not have acute episodes, the less good are the chances of recovery. These can be taken as guidelines only, and the experienced doctor knows best how to weigh the presence of one factor against the presence or absence of another. The situation is made even more complicated by considering whether one is concerned with the immediate or short-term prognosis, as opposed to the outcome over an extended period of time, the long-term prognosis. Some conditions clear up very quickly (good short-term prognosis) but have a tendency to recur (poor long-term prognosis), whereas others may drag on over the months (poor short-term prognosis) but may not recur (good long-term prognosis).

It may be very difficult to distinguish the episode of a disorder which is going to be one of a series of such relapses leading to a progressive decline into the chronic state from that which is going to be a single isolated incident never to recur, or, if it does, not to lead to progressive deterioration. Only by taking all the factors of the social situation, the clinical history and clinical features into account can the doctor hazard any guess, and even at best it remains a guess. There are no certainties in this game of chance. It is hoped, however, that as diagnostic tools become more selective and efficient we will be able to forecast with ever greater accuracy what the outcome is likely to be.

Schizophrenic-like States

Although the concept of schizophrenia still lacks clarity, precision and agreement, and although the clinical picture of the disorder is so varied in its presentation, there are a number of conditions which can be mistaken for this disorder but which are known to be definitely different from it. It is as important for persons suffering from these disorders not to be classed as schizophrenics as it is for schizophrenic patients not to be mistaken for them. All these disorders involve to a greater or lesser extent odd behaviour with which the observer may find it difficult to identify, but not all these disorders would be considered to be examples of 'madness'.

(a) *Adolescent identity crisis*: it has now been recognised that, as part of the period of adjustment between infancy and adulthood called adolescence, discovering who one is, that is establishing an identity, is a very important feature. Some young people experience an extreme form of loss of personal identity which leads to a picture very like schizophrenia. They both occur in young people, but the identity crisis responds well to psychological management such as psychotherapy, and the person recovers without any ongoing damage to his personality structure. This condition is temporary and essentially of a good prognosis if recognised and adequately treated.

(b) *Depersonalisation states*: this psychological experience is usually the result either of accumulating anxiety or of fatigue. It can happen to anyone, and is frequently experienced but usually not talked about for fear of being labelled mad by others. The person feels somehow changed in himself, but still keeps a grip on his own identity, unlike the schizophrenic. Many people have the feeling of coming out of themselves and observing dispassionately what they themselves are doing. There is a split in the perception of self but not such a primitive one as occurs in schizophrenia.

This condition is associated with what is called *déjà vu*, that is the experience that one has been in a place before when one knows that one has not, or that one knows what is going to happen next although one knows there are no real means of being sure of this. Various explanations have been devised to explain this experience, including the theory of reincarnation and the concept of spiral time: namely, that we all have been here before in a previous dimension of the time spiral and thus can 'remember' what happened last time we were here.

(c) *Toxic states*: in which the patient experiences vivid visual hallucinations and may misinterpret what is going on around him to a delusional extent. Such patients are usually terrified and actively paranoid. Delirium tremens is a good example of this state, brought on by acute alcohol poisoning. The condition has a good prognosis and remits as the cause of the toxic state is removed.

(d) *Epileptic psychosis*: again the patient who suffers from epileptic attacks may feel changed in himself in subtle ways and have vivid visual hallucinations, often of an apocalyptic nature. He may be impulsive and violent, and his emotional response may be incongruous. These potentially dangerous states respond well to treatment of the primary epilepsy.

(e) *Ganser states*: these are conditions of simulated madness in persons undergoing detention or in a penal setting. The person gives approximate answers to questions, appearing to be mad in order to escape from the consequences of his actions. In cases where the motivation is clearly conscious, the person can be said to be malingering, but in others the person may be unaware of what is happening because part of his psychic life is split off from the rest in a hysterical-like way.

(*f*) *Othello syndrome*: these are cases of morbid jealousy almost amounting to paranoia. The husband is convinced that his wife is having an affair often on the most flimsy evidence, and then sets out to prove his convictions in the way of a self-fulfilling prophesy. Marks on the skin, alterations of voice or gesture are all taken as proof of infidelity. If she protests her innocence, it is because she is guilty; if she does not, that is ample proof in itself. The victim is trapped in the fantasies of her husband and cannot win whatever she does.

(*g*) *States of possession*: these are rare in clinical practice and usually occur in a ritualistic setting. The sufferer believes that his body has been taken over and is controlled by the spirit of another person. Occasionally schizophrenics will claim that they are possessed as an explanation for their symptoms.

(*h*) *Schizoid personality*: by this is meant persons who are of a shy and retiring personality. They avoid people and show little overt emotion. Their psychic life is an inward-turning introspective one. They are threatened by intimacy and prefer things to persons. Many are involved in intellectual and philosophical thought and may believe that others are persecuting them. Because of their retreat from reality, their social efficiency can deteriorate and they may withdraw even further from others as a result. This is a type of person, and does not signify an illness.

(*i*) *Model psychoses*: these are toxic psychotic states induced by chemical substances called hallucinogens, whose principal effect is to produce confusion and vivid hallucinations. These artificially induced psychoses have been extensively studied to see if they reveal anything about the nature of naturally occurring psychosis. Mescalin and LSD (lysergic acid diethylamide) are two commonly studied hallucinogens.

(*i*) *Hypnagogic states*: these are vivid hallucinatory experiences which occur at the moment of falling asleep. The sufferer is in the grip of a kind of waking dream. A similar condition occurs as the person is waking up. The experience is terrifying and more common than suspected, because again people do not like to talk about it for fear that they are going out of their minds. It is caused by a change in the process whereby successive parts of the brain are inhibited during the onset or waking out of sleep. As a higher part of the brain is inhibited, lower parts which it normally holds in check, as it were, escape into temporary overactivity until they in turn are inhibited.

(*k*) *Sensory deprivation*: it is known that, where external stimulation to the brain is cut down, the person loses a sense of personal identity and orientation. As sensory deprivation progresses, the individual becomes confused and then enters a stage of hallucination. It is as if the brain was trying to provide external stimulation by projecting outwards sensory experiences. This occurs in the techniques of political thought reform (brain washing) and in research projects into how the brain functions under conditions of stress. This had a practical significance in that it could limit space exploration over large distances where the space crew will be relatively inactive for long periods and lacking in a variety of external stimulation.

(*l*) *Infantile autism*: this is a rare development condition of children in which they fail to learn how to establish and maintain meaningful relationships. The child speaks of himself in the third person much like the commentary voices of the schizophrenic. Such children withdraw into themselves, fail to make social contact and may show violent outbursts of impulsive aggression. They are to be distinguished from the equally rare condition of childhood schizophrenia and the much commoner condition of mental retardation or subnormality.

All these conditions have features in common with the schizophrenias, but each is quite different from that disorder and have a different mode of causation, management and prognosis. The important thing is that the condition be recognised for what it is, and that it is not confused with a schizophrenic psychosis.

What is the Cause?

In any science description is easier than both interpretation and deduction. Although it is difficult to agree what constitutes schizophrenia, it is relatively easy to describe the different elements of what is commonly recognised as schizophrenic behaviour and experience. What is difficult is to be sure of what is the causation of the disorders. It is in this area that there is the greatest disagreement among the various workers in the field.

In a condition which is relatively common, and so protean in its manifestations, it is hardly surprising that there should be so many theories as to its causation. The difficulty is not in having too many theories, but in deciding how relevant each one is and, if it is relevant, how it relates to all the other relevant theories. There has been a long debate in medicine on the relative effect of nature and nurture on the causation of many disorders.

Is the condition due to an inherited factor (nature), or is it due to some influence which plays upon the organism subsequent to its conception (nurture)? This age-old debate has been settled, by agreeing that in no condition is the disorder causally due exclusively to either nature or nurture but is due to both, and the debate continues as to how great is the contribution of each to the whole. And so it is with this complex condition which we have called schizophrenia.

It will be easier when we study the theories of causation if they are grouped under the three great conceptual models: the somatic or organic causations, the psychological causations and the social causations.

1 Theories of somatic causation

(a) *Genetical theory:* this suggests that there is a specific gene or group of genes which causes schizophrenia. A gene is a package of inherited material in the chromosome which not only initiates and controls the growth of the different parts of the body but may also be responsible for disorders and diseases. The evidence for this genetical theory lies in the increased incidence of schizophrenia among relatives of certain patients and in certain studies of twins. This aspect of increased incidence has already been discussed under the heading 'Incidence and Prevalence'. A simple gene explanation for schizophrenia is too naïve, and what is probably inherited is the constitutional disposition to schizophrenia which is then released by other factors.

(b) *Somatotype theory:* a somatotype is a classification of bodily form from measurement. People fall into three main types: long and thin (ectomorph), short and fat (endomorph), and medium but muscular (mesomorph). Earlier studies suggested that schizophrenia was commoner among the ectomorphs, the long, thin individuals. Patients in hospital studies were described as asthenic (lean) with long tapering, often cyanosed (blue-coloured), extremities. A link was thought to exist between somatotype and genetical predisposition.

(c) *Brain theories:* brain damage usually results in epilepsy (fits), but it can also occasionally 'release' a schizophrenic-like state in predisposed individuals. This would be an example of secondary or symptomatic schizophrenia. The electroencephalogram (EEG) is the recorded pattern of electrical activity in the brain, which varies with specific situations and specific disorders. It was hoped that studies of the EEG patterns of schizophrenics would reveal abnormalities. Various workers at various times have reported various abnormal patterns, but no consistent 'schizophrenic' pattern has ever been found. However, that the EEG can be abnormal is significant and supports the theory that there is altered brain functioning in the schizophrenias. Likewise routine post mortem studies of the brains of schizophrenic patients failed to reveal any specific anatomical or pathological change.

In epilepsy, where there is both an abnormal EEG and often gross brain damage, schizophrenic-like states do occur (the epileptic psychoses), but these differ in particular ways as we have already seen. But once again the fact that a schizophrenic-like disorder occurs in another condition known to be due to a physical disorder of the brain gives strong support to the suggestion that schizophrenia could likewise have an organic basis.

(d) *Metabolic theory*: the brain is very sensitive to metabolic change, that is change in those naturally occurring chemicals which are carried to it in the blood stream. The brain relies on oxygen and glucose for its main fuel to support neuronal activity. Research has suggested that in schizophrenics there is a change in the rate of oxygen uptake and the utilisation of glucose. Thyroid hormone is important for maintained cerebral activity and a particularly rare form of schizophrenia known as Gjessing's catatonia was shown by him to be due to altered thyroid function. Also, it is clinically observed that there is an increased incidence of schizophrenic breakdown in the puerperium (period after childbirth) and in the menopause (the change of life). In both of these periods there are marked changes in the levels of female sex hormones and it is thought that this imbalance might trigger off predisposed individuals.

(e) *Neuro-chemical theory*: the actual function of the nerve tissue (transmission of nervous impulses) depends on very small quantities of powerful chemicals which operate at the junction of one nerve cell with another. It is known that these chemical transmitter substances can be inhibited by drugs, or be allowed to act much longer than they would usually do because a naturally occurring deactivating mechanism has been blocked. In these circumstances, states very like schizophrenia can occur. Also the drugs known as hallucinogens (hallucination makers), such as mescaline and lysergic acid diethylamide, cause artificial psychotic states (the model psychoses) by altering the action of these transmitter substances. It is now believed by some workers that a failure in the chain of generation of these transmitters leads to the production of intermediary substances which then act as naturally occurring hallucinogens. Increasing psychological stress leads to a greater metabolic turnover and thus there is a link between psychological events and physical change in the brain.

Recent research caused great excitement when a 'pink spot' was found on the test paper during the chemical electrophoretic examination of the urine of a schizophrenic patient. The spot was identified as a mescaline-like substance— DMPE. This was a clear-cut physical demonstration of one of the altered transmitter substances. Unfortunately, as has happened with many chemical theories, not all schizophrenics give a pink spot, and in addition the pink spot has been found in other conditions not related to schizophrenia. However, there is enough evidence once more to suggest that, in some cases of schizophrenia at least, there are demonstrable biochemical changes and this paves the way for further research, which could have far-reaching repercussions not only in terms of aetiology or causation but also in terms of chemical control of the disorder.

2 Theories of psychological causation

(a) *Pre-morbid personality type:* just as a particular body formation was shown to be more associated with schizophrenia than others, so studies of large numbers of schizoohrenic patients have shown an overall representation of certain preceding personality types. Two types have been found in particular: the schizoid personality already described, and the sensitive personality, those people who react badly to all kinds of stresses both physical and psychological. If it is accepted that genetic inheritance plays a part in the development of personality, a genetic predisposition for schizophrenia is once more supported. There is, however, a hidden difficulty here—people with abnormal personalities are likely to get themselves into abnormal situations, and thus expose themselves to more stress than other people might experience, and the question is raised as to whether any schizophrenia is due directly to the underlying personality defect or due to the increased stress situations which these people find themselves in.

(b) *Ego psychology theory*: this is the psychology of the self; that unique experience of me as a person, as different from all other persons, and also the experience of me as a living person different from inanimate objects which may surround me. In the beginning the child has his existence centred around his mother, who meets all his needs. He begins to feel himself as different and separate from her when his needs are not met, and he feels hungry and frustrated. He begins at a primitive level to distinguish between self and non-self. Later he incorporates his father and brothers and sisters into his psychology of persons. The more people he can recognise, the more he can recognize himself as being different and separate from them. He begins to establish what are called ego boundaries, that is an awareness of where he himself stops and others who are not him begin. He begins to separate out people and objects, and to see them against a background, in front of which life is acted out. This process of assembling a batch of stimuli into a meaningful whole, which is perceived in relationship to other meaningful wholes, is called forming a gestalt. I know who I am because I have intact ego boundaries, and I am aware of myself in a gestalt sense, in relationship to the background around me which is not me.

In schizophrenia, ego boundaries become frayed, blurred and fractured so that the patient loses a sense of himself because he feels that he diffuses out of himself into his surroundings. He loses a sense of self and of non-self. He also loses the ability to form gestalts, and the figure, foreground and background become interchangeable. Thus patients are terrified of being swallowed up literally by other people, by being absorbed into them. They also talk literally of becoming someone else, but of being themselves at the same time. They believe that they can influence other people by influencing themselves. One patient who played football believed that when he hurt his own leg all the members of the opposing team were hurt in the same way. He had lost a sense of himself and was being merged with his opponents. Another patient felt that evil came out of her and caused a national catastrophe at a distance. These patients have lost a sense of personal identity and are being absorbed into the universal identity.

(c) *Perceptual filter theory:* there is a continuous bombardment of our brains by a flood of incoming stimuli from our five senses. If all these stimuli had immediate access to the computer within the cental nervous system, the 'machine' would fail because of information overload. In simpler words, we can only pay real attention to one thing at a time, and handle only a limited amount of information. The 'perceptual filter' is a suggested mechanism whereby the brain selects the stimuli in terms of relative priority and only pays attention to those of a selected modality. This is why, when we are concentrating on our reading, we are not aware of the clock ticking in the room or the feel of the chair beneath us. The sensitivity of a particular modality can be pre-selected. Thus an anxious mother awakes at once at the slightest whimper from her baby but does not 'hear' the sound of the wind in the trees outside.

It is suggested that, in schizophrenia, the perceptual filter breaks down and consciousness is flooded with too much information at once. Although in a clinical setting schizo-

hrenic patients look very flat and non-responsive, they are in
act very sensitive to what is happening around them. They
ick up every subtle nuance of meaning and of expression.
They are overwhelmed into passivity by the bombardment of
mpressions from their environment which surrounds them.
This could be an explanation of why their thinking is so fragmented.

(d) *Unconscious anxiety theory*: in dreams, conflicts and fears
which have been repressed in the waking state emerge from
the unconscious mind in symbols and express themselves.
Dreaming thus has a curative function, allowing the repressed
emotions to be catharted in a disguised form. The conscious
ego cannot tolerate primitive anxieties to do with existence and
survival, and sanity is threatened when anxiety from the unconscious percolates through into consciousness.

It is suggested that the psychosis of schizophrenia is a kind
of perpetual waking dream in which the control of those deep
primitive anxieties has been lost. Certainly, there is a great
similarity between the symbols of dreams and the symbols
which schizophrenics show in their art.

(e) *The Oedipal theory*: During adolescence the young person
begins to be attracted to members of the opposite sex. This
means that at the same time he comes into active competition
with his peer group and members of his own sex. There then
develops a particular conflict with older members of his own
sex who are set in authority over him, especially his father.
The young person wishes to be free from the restraints of
what he regards as an arbitrary authority. Because he has
hostile feelings towards the authority figures, he presupposes
that they in turn will have hostile feelings towards him, but because of their authority they have more power to act out their
vengeance on the young man. The same situation develops
between girls and their mothers, but there the conflict is not
over openly declared power and authority but much more
about sexuality and the arts of seduction. This oedipal conflict

has to be resolved in some way, and most families do so by letting their young people go free to establish themselves as new adults in wider society. The young people can then come back at a later date with less conflict, because each side of the struggle has gained a new composure and confidence in the meanwhile.

It is believed that if the oedipal conflict is not resolved there can only be a limited number of alternative stratagems left to the young people. They can go on fighting into ripe old age (the angry young men who never grow up); they can give in by becoming totally passive and submit themselves to the will of their parents; they can opt-out by killing themselves (suicide) and they can opt-out by becoming mad. It is as if the real world is too painful to live in, so they retreat from reality into a fantasy world of their own making, where they have 'magical' power over objects and persons around them. An unresolved oedipal conflict is a potent source of the kind of unconscious primitive anxiety we have already discussed.

(f) *Double bind theory*: a bind is an uncomfortable influence which one has over another. The sociologist Gregory Bateson examined the interactions between schizophrenic children and their parents, and showed that these families manifested a lot of what he called 'double bind' patterns. By this he meant that the parents continually involved the children in double bind situations which had the following components. Firstly, a primary injunction—'do this'—then a secondary cancelling negative injunction—'don't do this'—and finally a demand that the child does not escape out of the bind but responds in some way. If a parent says to a child 'I order you to disobey me', the child cannot respond in any way which will please the parent. He literally cannot win and parental displeasure and probable punishment are inevitable. This kind of communication pattern occurs not only in schizophrenic families. We may have experienced how intolerable this kind of situation is: we are warned that we will be punished if we behave in a certain way; we are then dealt with in such a way that we can only respond in the forbidden way, or even if we do not we are charged that we have, and the inevitable punishment ensues. We are incensed by the injustice and the 'madness' of the whole situation.

Bateson does not say that double binding is exclusive to schizophrenic families, but that this type of interaction pattern seems to be more common in such families. Thus there is a sense in which the parents can be said to drive their children mad. There is only one stratagem whereby the child can escape and that is to retreat into a fantasy world in which his double-binding parents have no existence, or where he can in turn exercise magical power over them.

Other workers have objected to the suggestion in this theory that it is the double binding which gives rise to schizophrenia, and have suggested the alternative hypothesis that families develop this kind of relationship when there is a schizophrenic member already in the family. This theory overlaps into the next group of theories of causation.

3 Social theories of causation

(a) *Schizophrenogenic mother theory*: in the early days of sociological research, workers looked at the kind of mothers who had schizophrenic children and compared them to mothers whose children were not schizophrenic. A pattern of maternal behaviour emerged. Mothers of the schizophrenics showed two characteristics. Firstly, they were more demanding and rejecting of their children—they asked more of them, and then rejected the children if they failed to come up to parental expectation. Secondly, they were more inconsistent in their attitudes to the children—one minute they might be declaring how much they loved their children, and the next they would be cool, off-handed and hostile. Faced with this type of mother, the child does not know where he stands, but he knows perhaps one thing and one thing only, and that is that he is unacceptable as he is to his mother, however much she may speak with her words to the contrary.

T.Y.S.—5

Once more it is not said that such behaviour is exclusive to schizophrenogenic mothers, but it is found in them more often than to be expected on a general average. It has also been argued as to which comes first—does this kind of mother produce a schizophrenic child, or is this an understandable maternal reaction to the frustrations of trying to bring up a psychotic child? The debate continues and suggests many areas for further research.

(b) *Family interaction theory:* with the development of socio-logical techniques suitable for analysing how people relate to each other in groups, studies have been made of whole families in which one member is schizophrenic and significant patterns of interaction have been looked for. If specific patterns are found, there could be two explanations: the first being that the interaction pattern has contributed to one member becoming schizophrenic (as with the theory of the schizophrenogenic mother), and the second being that the interaction pattern is a result of one member already being schizophrenic. We have met this dichotomy before. Studies have been made particularly of the relationship of the parental generation to the child generation to try to find out if there is any validity in the suggestion that people can literally 'drive one another mad'.

It is one of the prerequisites for sanity that others should validate our communications. This does not mean that they have necessarily to agree with everything we say, but that they should convey the feeling that they consider that our com-munications are valid or meaningful. Nothing is more disturb-ing than to have all your communications returned to you as invalid, meaningless or irrelevant. This situation becomes all the more disturbing if, as we try to find out why our communications are invalid, we are constantly met with the assertion that they are, and that we should learn how to communicate properly, but at the same time we are denied all the means of finding out how to make them valid.

It is suggested that in schizophrenic families particularly this kind of miscommunication is more prevalent. There are families in which there appear to be good communications—a mutuality between the various members of the family—but on careful scrutiny we find that this is a pseudomutuality only— there is an insistence that communication is taking place to hide the fact that it is not, and an equal collusion to deny that deception is taking place. This is thought to be one way of driving people mad. In other families double binding is the characteristic method of communication—yet another way of saying that communication is taking place in order to deny that it is not.

In other families it is not so much covert and latent communication that is at fault as distortion of role playing within the family. It is customary for parents to look after children and for sexual relationships not to develop between members of the same family. In some schizophrenic families these rules have been shown to be broken. A rift develops between the parents, and then intense collusions are built up of two people against a third. Classically, the father is devalued, excluded from the family even, and then the mother seduces her own son into replacing his father. He, the son, is now called upon to look after his mother. There may be no actual sexual contact, but the mother acts towards her son as if he were her lover, the theme of D. H. Lawrence's book *Sons and Lovers*. It is suggested that it is the confusion which comes from this distortion and inversion of roles in the family which is the basis for a developing psychosis.

These are only tentative hypotheses but they furnish suggestions for further research. It would appear from studies already conducted that inconsistency of communication, denial of collusions contrary to the evidence and inversions of roles invalidate a person's feeling of indentity and of being at home in his environment. This could be the beginning of the loosening of grasp upon an uncomfortable reality and a compensatory flight into psychotic fantasies.

(c) *Role playing theory*: this is used in the analysis of family interaction types, but can apply equally well to relationships outside the home. It is presupposed that each of us needs a pay-off to continue to behave in a given way. We are motivated by a reward. In social terms, the reward is often simply being recognised and accepted as a member of the group. To belong to the group, we must behave in a way in which the group expects us to behave. If we behave in an unpredictable way we disturb others, and if this pattern of relating persists we ultimately will be excluded from the group. All of us want to belong and to do so we have to conform to the group expectations of us.

For various reasons a person may be expected to be mad—he may look mad, there may be a history of madness in the family, someone may have stated once that he was mad, and particularly if the group needs a 'madman' to be a scapegoat (someone to blame for everything that goes wrong) the only way that this person may be acceptable to the group is literally to become 'mad'. In this way society creates its 'madmen' and families groom a member for a career in 'schizophrenia'.

(d) *The social drift theory*: It has been observed that schizophrenics congregate in poorer districts of large cities and are to be found in greater proportion in the lower grades of the social classes. It was originally thought that it was the stresses of the poor life which caused schizophrenia in predisposed individuals.

It is now known that these observations are the result of schizophrenia rather than a cause of it. Because the schizophrenic loses social skills and becomes steadily socially incompetent as a result of his disorder, he will not be able to perform skilled jobs and so will drift down the occupational scale. Because he can earn relatively little, he can only afford to live where housing is cheaper. Researchers have also shown that whereas schizophrenics are over-represented in the lower social grades, the families from which they come are distributed normally. This further confirms that it is not the nature of the family of origin which gives rise to the schizophrenia in social terms, but it is becoming a schizophrenic that leads to the patient drifting down the social classes.

Related to this are the observations that schizophrenics have been found more than would be expected in lonely parts of the world, such as the north of Scandinavia, and in lonely jobs, such as the Merchant Navy. Once more this is not a cause of the disorder as once was thought, but a consequence of it. Because schizophrenics do not find it easy to relate warmly to other human beings, they are attracted to areas of relative social isolation where they are left much to their own devices and can relate more comfortably to things rather than to persons.

In trying to relate all these theories of causation—somatic, psychological and social—the attempt to find a single cause has been abandoned in favour of a multiple causation. In other words, schizophrenia, or more correctly the schizophrenias, is not due to any one cause but is due to a number of inter-relating factors. Some factors *predispose* the individual to behave in a certain way, while other factors *precipitate* the appearance of the disorder.

Just how complicated this can be is shown in a book called *The Genain Quadruplets* by David Rosenthal. Quadruplets are four children grown from one maternal germ cell, and so all have in theory the same genetical make-up. Of the Genain quadruplets, three became obviously schizophrenic, but the fourth did not. For this reason the family was extensively studied over a number of years, and an attempt was made to tease out all the factors operating in this family. If schizophrenia has a genetical basis, quadruplets all brought up together should either not be schizophrenic or all should be schizophrenic. How one could differ from the expected is the basis of this fascinating book, which seeks to show the complex relationship of all these possible theories of causation.

In a sense we both know too much and too little about schizophrenia. We know too much in that we have so many possible explanatory hypotheses. We know too little because we do not know as yet how to integrate fully all these possible explanations and we still know too little about what the condition really is for which we are trying to find a meaningful and creative explanation. An explanation is necessary not simply to satisfy our curiosity, but to be the only rational basis on which to mount effective programmes of management.

Part 3

The Management of Schizophrenia

'Though this be madness, yet there is method in it.'

William Shakespeare: *Hamlet*

Introduction

In psychiatry deviant behaviour poses a particularly difficult conflict for the doctor. When he is asked by society on its behalf to deal with a deviant person, the doctor can never be quite sure whether he is being asked to treat the patient for his own sake, or whether he is being asked to treat the deviant for the sake of society so that the one-time deviant can cease to be an irritation and perhaps optimumly be accepted into the group once more.

The choice is between what is best for the individual and what is best for the group. If the doctor can perform both tasks simultaneously, as often he can, the outcome is a happy one, but sometimes these two aims are in conflict and cannot be resolved. What is then described as 'treatment' of the individual is in fact thinly disguised 'control' of the individual for society's sake.

If the doctor wishes to be true to his patient he will wish to help him to develop his full potentialities, but he may in doing so increase the tension between the patient and his group, for example his family. The emergence of the deviant behaviour may be an attempt to achieve autonomy and self-determination within the group. If the doctor then helps the patient to a greater degree of individuality, he may be even more unacceptable to the group. If he, by his management, makes the patient more conforming, the doctor may be taking away from the patient what little autonomy and self-determination he once may have had.

Management therefore of the deviant person has to proceed cautiously between this Scylla and Charybdis, at times sacrificing one for the benefit of the other but at other times reversing the process. Knowing which way to go at any given moment cannot be taught as a science, but is the very art of medicine at its best.

Schizophrenia is a form of deviant behaviour, as we have seen, and it will be helpful if we look at the management of the schizophrenic patient from three different viewpoints— the management of the patient in hospital, the management of the patient in the therapeutic community, which may be either in hospital or outside it, and the managment of the patient in the wider community.

In hospital

Schizophrenic patients are admitted to hospital for a variety of reasons. Behind all these is the assumption, explicit or otherwise, that either the patient can no longer cope in the community or society can no longer cope with him. The most common reason for admission is that the patient's disorder has reached such an acute stage of disorganisation that he can no longer look after himself.

He may have been unemployed for some time, simply roaming the streets and being out late at night. He may have failed to bother to eat or to keep himself clean. He may have been observed talking to his hallucinatory voices, or may have suddenly turned on someone in response to delusional ideas. Usually there is a period of growing concern about him and then his behaviour goes beyond an unspoken but certainly real level of social tolerance, and the state of 'something having to be done' is reached. This going beyond a socially acceptable level of disfunction may be a very subtle thing. There may in fact be very little change in the patient's actual symptomatology, but his circumstances may have changed in a direction in which there is believed to be a real loss or potential loss of control. Single middle-aged male schizophrenics often have to come into hospital when their mother dies, not because they are necessarily worse from a medical viewpoint, but because it is felt in the community that the patient is now in greater risk or that the community is in greater risk from him.

The reasons for admission may arise slowly and insidiously, or they may occur abruptly and chaotically, as for example when a schizophrenic suddenly becomes actively hallucinated and attacks a person or group of persons, believing them to be his persecutors. The public will then turn to someone in the role of trouble-shooter to get the schizophrenic into hospital. This may be couched in terms of 'it being for his own good in the long run' but is often only a thinly disguised manoeuvre to get a disturbingly deviant person out of the community and out of harm's way. The public may call on a police officer if it is in the street, or the general practitioner if it is in the home.

Whoever is called, the situation may be relatively easy if the schizophrenic is willing to go into hospital. But often, especially if he is acutely paranoid, he may see being put into hospital as a trick on the part of his enemies to 'put him away' and will refuse steadfastly to go. At this juncture the question of *compulsory admission* must be considered.

The law generally is designed to protect the interests of the individual, but in certain circumstances the rights of the individual may be thought to be subordinate to the rights of the community. In this case the schizophrenic may be thought to be too disturbed to make a valid judgment as to what is in his best interest, i.e. to accept medical treatment in hospital, or it is judged that he should be controlled against his wishes for the protection of others.

The Mental Health Act of 1959, which embodies the law as it applies to the control and management of psychiatrically disordered persons, states that when a patient is diagnosed by a doctor as suffering from such a degree of mental illness that he is unable to make valid judgments about himself and others, he may be detained compulsorily in a hospital for his own protection and/or for the protection of others. A general practitioner wishing to invoke a section of the Mental Health Act has to obtain the agreement of a near relative and is aided in the execution of the Mental Health Act by a Mental Welfare Officer, a mental health social worker especially appointed and trained for the purpose.*

There are two sections which may be applied for: a Section 29 order, which is an emergency order that allows the patient to be detained for up to seventy-two hours, and a Section 25 order, which allows the patient to be detained for observation and treatment for up to twenty-eight days. The latter order has to be signed by a doctor especially recognised to be experienced in the diagnosis of mental disorders.

There is a further Section 26 order, which can be applied once a patient is in the hospital, which allows the patient to be detained for treatment up to one year in the first instance. This order would only be used in exceptional circumstances where all other methods had been tried and had been shown to have failed.

Generally, the hope is that patients will be able to see the wisdom of accepting treatment and will voluntarily place themselves in the care of the hospitals. This is to do away with the old fear that once someone is committed to a psychiatric hospital he never comes out again. At the present time, due to an enlightened approach to the care of the psychiatrically disturbed, less than 10 per cent of all patients admitted to psychiatric hospitals come in under a section of the Mental Health Act. The majority of patients are said to be admitted informally and agree voluntarily to accept treatment.

Once a patient has agreed to accept treatment or is made the subject of a detention order, the choice is whether to admit

* Since the Social Services Act of 1972 the functions of the erstwhile Mental Welfare Officer have now been taken on by all social workers recognised for this purpose.

aim to the psychiatric unit of a general hospital or to the local psychiatric hospital. The choice is often a theoretical one because at present not all large towns have psychiatric units in the general hospital, but the intention for the future is to build more of these. Where one is available the schizophrenic can often be treated quite satisfactorily there, and be discharged for follow-up care in his community after a stay of two to three months.

For most patients at present, admission means going to the local psychiatric hospital. These are based in catchment areas serving a large population either in a city or in a sparsely populated rural area such as Cambridgeshire and the Isle of Ely. Each psychiatric hospital—the old mental hospital or county mental asylum—has a long historical connection with the catchment area, and although old fears and prejudices still survive the fact of being admitted for treatment is less distressing because of the improved understanding of what such an admission means to the patient and to his family, and because of the great improvements in the treatment available.

Just as we have divided the views of causation of schizophrenia into the three great areas of physical, psychological and social, so the management of the schizophrenic in hospital can best be described under the headings of physical treatment, psychological treatment and social treatment.

(a) Physical treatment

This is naturally based on the conception of schizophrenia as being a medical disorder with a physical basis, or at least having a symptomatology which can be modified by physical means. The physical means used are drugs, ECT and leucotomy.

Drugs

A drug is a chemical substance which when taken into the body effects some change. In this case the change which it is hoped to effect is either to modify the influence of the causal factors or to suppress the clinical features. Whichever is achieved, the patient will feel better in himself and it is hoped that he will be more effective in his behaviour.

The principal discovery in this area was that the major tranquillisers (drugs which quieten turbulent emotions without significantly altering consciousness) had what was considered by some to be an anti-psychotic effect. The debate is still current whether these drugs attack the primary process or act more by suppressing symptoms. These drugs belong to the class of the *phenothiazine derivatives* and are known by various names—chlorpromazine (Largactil), thioridazine (Melleril), trifluoperazine (Stelazine) and so on. It must be stressed that these drugs are used for their tranquillising effect in conditions other than schizophrenia and that in schizophrenia they have to be given in larger doses. One of the side-effects of these drugs is that they produce a condition of stiffness and tremor of the muscles known as Parkinsonism, and so have to be combined with *anti-Parkinson drugs* such as benzhexol (Artane) or benztropine (Cogentin).

Many schizophrenics are depressed in spirit and, as we have seen, disturbance of mood is one of the cardinal features. This can often be helped by *antidepressant drugs* which act as psychic energisers, mood elevators or mood correctors.

Such drugs belong to two main classes: the tricyclic drugs such as imipramine (Tofranil) and the monoamine-oxidase inhibitors such as phenelzine (Nardil). It has been found in clinical experience that, while the tricyclic antidepressants can be given safely to schizophrenics on their own, the monoamine-oxidase inhibitors are best combined with a phenothiazine tranquilliser, otherwise they can 'light up' and make worse a schizophrenic disorder. Likewise, psychic energisers of the amphetamine class such as Drinamyl are best avoided for a similar reason. Schizophrenics, like all of us, are prone to anxiety and stress, and at times do not sleep as a result. They will be helped by *sedatives* of the barbiturate type such as butobarbitone (Soneryl) or pentobarbitone sodium (Nembutal). Because these are habit-forming, other non-barbiturate *hypnotics* such as dichloralphenazone (Welldorm) or nitraze-pam (Mogadon) may be used instead.

Recently a great technical development has been the introduction of *slow release phenothiazine drugs* which can be injected in a depot form. The patient has an injection from his doctor or district nurse and once the dose is stabilised he may only need an injection once every five or six weeks. This is of particular help when the patients are not willing, or do not remember, to take their drugs. The phenothiazine so far used for this purpose is fluphenazine and is marketed as Moditen or Modecate. Parkinsonism is likely to occur with these injections as well, so that an anti-Parkinson drug has to be taken, especially in the week immediately following the injection.

This technique has cut down the amount of nursing time needed to dispense other tablets three or four times a day, and has resulted in many chronic schizophrenics being able to be discharged out of hospital into the community. Here they attend their own family doctor or see the district nurse at home or in the health centre. Some psychiatric hospitals have now established Moditen Clinics on an out-patient basis.

Another completely different kind of drug which is used in schizophrenia is *insulin*. This is the naturally occurring substance produced in the pancreas gland which helps to move glucose out of the blood stream into the tissues.

We have already noted that glucose is one of the main fuel sources of energy for the nerve cell. In the early days *deep insulin therapy* was given. This method was devised by Sakel in Vienna in the 1930s and the beneficial response in schizophrenia was empirical. That means that no one knew quite how it worked, only that it did work. In this technique, a team of workers gave the patients in a group setting such large doses of insulin that they sank into a coma from which they were subsequently roused by means of a glucose infusion.

This was a potentially dangerous treatment and it is now known that the benefit to the schizophrenic came not so much from the chemical effect of the insulin comas as from the intensive group therapy which the technique involved. For this reason the technique has now been abandoned in favour of *modified insulin therapy* in which only a small dose of insulin is given, enough to cause a slight dizziness and sweating. The patient remains fully conscious and the treatment phase is terminated with a glucose drink.

This procedure mobilises glucose into the muscle stores so that the patient puts on weight and for a variety of reasons, both physical and psychological, feels much better in himself and in better morale.

Electroconvulsant therapy (ECT) is another empirical treatment for mental disorder discovered by von Meduna, again in the 1930s. He showed that convulsions (fits) chemically induced in patients resulted in clinical improvement. An electrical method of inducing convulsions was introduced later by two Italian psychologists Carletti and Bini.

It is unfortunate that the name of this treatment is so frightening to people because of their uneasy association of electricity, convulsions and the head. When it is properly administered to patients who have previously been given a general anaesthetic there is no unpleasantness at all and the method brings rapid relief to the patient. It is effective most where there are marked emotional changes, or where there is acute withdrawal, as in the stuporose state of catatonia.

The arguments again are raised as to whether this technique is primarily anti-psychotic, or whether in a non-specific way the stress which is induced at a metabolic level mobilises the body's defence mechanisms. ECT is often combined with the major tranquillisers and the antidepressants, for the suggestion is that ECT makes the organism more sensitive to these agents.

Prefrontal leucotomy

This is a surgical procedure in which some of the nerve fibres connecting the frontal areas of the brain with the deeper mid-brain areas are divided.

Once more it is an empirical treatment which was developed by the neuro-surgeon Egon Moniz after observing the change in personality experienced by patients who had received a naturally occurring brain injury. Moniz noticed that those patients who before the injury were tense, bitter and querulous became more relaxed and less caring, and thus less irritated by other people. He devised a technique, later developed by others, whereby under surgical control a similar relief of tension could be achieved. Because of the seriousness of this procedure and the fact that it is irreversible, it is only used in highly selected patients on whom all other methods have been used without lasting benefit and in whom there is a lot of tension.

Good results are obtained only when careful pre-operative selection is made. In the early days, the operation came into disrepute because of poor selection and because the technique used then was not as sophisticated as the methods of today. Often patients were changed but not necessarily for the better. It was said cynically that 'the patient feels much improved, but now it is his family who suffers'.

Good pre-operative selection and refined technique have meant that leucotomy still offers a valuable means of management of the disturbed and disturbing schizophrenic, who makes frequent and violent attacks upon others or upon himself, and of those patients tormented by tides of uncontrolled tension.

(b) Psychological treatment

This is based on the belief that psychological factors can both initiate and perpetuate a schizophrenic disorder. Psychological treatments are designed to reverse this process and to provide a secure milieu in which the anxiety and terror of the schizophrenic experience can be ameliorated and contained.

We have seen that the schizophrenic person is out of contact with himself and with others around him. He has not only lost the means of establishing contact but is also terrified of closeness. He is alienated both as a result of his disorder and as a means of coming to terms with his disorder. We have seen that the schizophrenic is overwhelmed by fears of losing what personal autonomy he may have left, and so protects himself by a flattened 'dead pan' exterior which does not invite others to make contact with him.

This external flattening had been thought to reflect a similar internal state, but psychological tests of the kind already described by Mr Robertson show us that the inner psychic world of the schizophrenic is more often characterised by chaos and turmoil than by emptiness or meaningless silence. It was the observation of this non-communicative exterior and the lack of response to human stimuli which led people to think of the schizophrenic as someone who would not be reached by communicative techniques such as psychotherapy.

Psychotherapy is the means by which one individual makes contact with another in a uniquely meaningful way and which, by the processes of analysis, interpretation and relationship formation, provides a new learning experience for the patient whereby he is able to outgrow his previous inefficient patterns of life responses and to put new more effective ones into operation.

By the nature of the disorder and by the nature of the largely incomprehensible conversations of the schizophrenic, schizophrenia was believed for long not to be suitable for psychotherapy. Emphasis was placed on physical treatments and other mechanical ways of changing the schizophrenic's responses to his environment.

One American psychotherapist, Frieda Fromm Reichmann, took a particular interest in young schizophrenic patients. By painfully patient work she established a method of making meaningful contact with her patients, with beneficial results. Her work was based on the belief that there was a healthy aspect of the inner person which could be contacted, and which could be trained to take over and control the less healthy aspect. Following her work, other psychotherapists have developed techniques for confronting the psychotic patient with reality and helping him to return to it.

John Rosen is associated with the technique of direct

analysis whereby the patient is made to confront his madness and is encouraged to lay aside psychotic ways of thinking, speaking and behaving. Not all psychiatrists agree with this technique and attribute much of the success of such approaches to the dynamism and dedicated interest of the therapist. This is a powerful element in any kind of therapy with people, separate from any significant action of the technique itself.

Whatever the psychotherapy used with schizophrenic patients, three elements are usually present:

(a) A supportive emotional experience in which the patient feels safe.
(b) A corrective feedback explicitly confronting the patient with the psychotic aspects of his behaviour.
(c) A gradual move towards reintegration of the fragmented self.

Psychotherapy can be conducted on an individual or group basis. In individual psychotherapy, the schizophrenic meets regularly with his therapist and the discussions between them are directed to the basic question of identity, 'Who am I?' In group therapy, a number of patients meet with one or more therapists and treatment follows lines of group discussions in which the patients speak to and question each other as much as the therapist. The basic question here is one of group identity, 'Who am I in relation to the others in this group?'

Individual therapy in more intense but the patient has only to relate to one other, whereas in the group setting the patient has a variety of persons with whom he can form a relationship. This is nearer to the real world in which most patients have to relate to a number of people—the 'generalised others' as opposed to the 'significant other' of a very close relationship of two persons. Any psychotherapy always tries to help the patient re-find himself and to re-enter effectively into the community life around him.

There are a number of other techniques with a psychological basis. R. D. Laing is a British psychiatrist who is concerned about the sociological significance of traditional psychiatry with its need to put persons into diagnostic classes such a 'schizophrenic'—'not schozophrenic'. He holds that the schizophrenic is one victim of a process of violence whereby powerful groups of people conspire against the autonomy of others by placing them in descriptive categories such as 'mad' or 'bad' as a way of exercising control over those of whom they disapprove.

Laing sees schizophrenia not so much as an illness as an attempt to escape out of these restraints. He has therefore constructed an experimental method of treatment in which schizophrenics are encouraged to become more psychotic to a stage of complete regression if necessary, believing that it is only by growing through the psychotic process that the person, who is elsewhere called a patient, is able to find and to capture his true self.

This approach involves a retreat to a phase of symbolic death of the disordered personality, which is then followed by a resurrection and rebirth to newness of life. This apporach is an empirical one based on a particular view of the kinds of social interactions which lead to schizophrenia. As a theoretical framework for explanation and treatment of schizophrenia, it goes counter to many of the traditional views of the psychiatric establishment, but it is worthy of consideration if in selected cases it does help schizophrenic persons to become whole again.

Family therapy is a logical development of the family interaction theory of causation. Even if certain family constellations were not thought to play any significant part in the genesis of the disorder, family relationships become disturbed as a result of one member of the family becoming psychotic and it would make sense therefore to try to deal with the problem at a family level. It is rarely practical to have a whole family in treatment, but if the patient is a young man or woman it is often possible to see the 'patient' together with the parents. This triangular relationship with three people will often allow many of the salient features of the basic family nteraction patterns to emerge. The principles behind family herapy with schizophrenics entail:

(a) Emphasising the problem at 'family level' rather than 'patient level'.

(b) Exposing the characteristic pattern of family communication or discommunication.

(c) Giving each person a fair hearing, and encouraging others to listen fairly to the content of the communications.

(d) Encouraging the emergence of alternative role expectations within the family.

Family therapy takes time, and there are hidden resistances to this approach both in the family and in the nominal patient, but it is worthwhile considering as it provides a dimension of care which will be missed if all the attention is focused on the patient as the sick person with problems, even when a family social history has been taken by a social worker.

Psychodrama is a highly specialised technique which makes use of role playing theory. Most of us would think that it is because we feel strong and brave that we become a soldier, or because we are gentle and sensitive that we become a poet, but role playing theory suggests that the truth is the other way round. When we are asked to play the part of being a soldier or being a poet, we assume the attributes of the part we play and, what is more, these attributes become assimilated into us and we make them peculiarly our own. We begin to behave and feel responsible when we are asked to play a responsible role. We have seen already that some people become mad because that is the group's expectation of them.

Psychodrama seeks to reverse this process: by prescribing the part to be played in an organised drama, it is hoped that the patient will incorporate into himself the feelings and attitudes he believes to be germane to that part. Psychodrama means both the free release of pent-up feelings (catharsis) and learning to identify with new roles and new role attributes. Patients are encouraged to give up the roles of 'psychiatric patient', 'madman', 'schizophrenic' and to try out other role such as 'successful husband', 'ambitious son' or 'competent daughter'. To be a good player one needs not only to be able to take on different roles but also to be able to play these role harmoniously with those that others are playing around one The mad are out of part with the rest of us; they insist on playing Lear when we are in the middle of Hamlet.

(c) Social treatment

In the days before the development of all the technical advances available to us now, psychiatric patients were given what was called *moral therapy*. This was an attempt to structure the patient's life in such a way that he became better able to fit in with others, and to be more efficient in a social sense as a result.

With schizophrenics, there was a vogue for *habit training*, which set out to instil into the disorganised patient a sense of time and a sense of programme. He was taught to be punctual, to keep himself clean and tidy, and to be able to perform simple repetitive tasks for which he was often given a reward.

Milieu therapy is a development of this approach in which it is recognised that the environment or milieu subtly influences how we feel about ourselves and other people, and that it is possible to alter people's feelings and behaviour by altering their milieu. It is not only a question of filling in time lest idle hands get up to mischief or the bored mind become a prey to depressing introspection, but really one of creating an atmosphere of expectancy in which the schizophrenic is able to act out a social role within the community of the psychiatric hospital and later within his own home.

Occupational therapy has moved away from the era of craft work such as weaving and basketry and into the era of *industrial therapy* in which firms subcontract projects to the hospital workshops where, in an atmosphere similar to a factory, the patients are paid according to the quantity of their output and the quality of their work. It is very important

hat the patient should identify with the project in hand, and
ee its relevance both for himself and for the community.

The work taken on can be quite sophisticated—from the
imple assembly of ball-point pens and television aerials to
omplex electronic wiring. When a patient is part of a team on
joint assembly, he learns not only how to do his own part of
he job for which he is rewarded but, more important, how
o relate most effectively to the rest of his team. He is in-
olved in a corporate effort in which his contribution is
aluable not only to himself but also to the team as a whole.

Recreational therapy seeks to help the patient develop any
reative talents within him. We have already looked at the
cope and value of art, but patients also do play reading and
lay acting. They organise concerts and debates, group
liscussions and team quizzes. Even running a social evening
or patients from another ward helps the patient to escape
rom the tyranny of his own preoccupations and become
ware of the existence and needs of others.

Finally, techniques of *socialisation* are used to bring the
atient out of the hospital into the community, and the
ommunity to the patient inside the hospital.

It has been said, with some truth, that the walls around the
lder mental hospitals were built as much to keep the public
ut as the patients in. For each group it was convenient to
ave the other as a scapegoat —'It's not really us that's at fault,
t's them in there, or them out there.'

Many hospitals now arrange outings to places of interest—
heatres, cinemas and museums—with talks beforehand to
elp the patients understand better what they are going to
ee. There are outings to the seaside or country for picnics
when the weather is fine. These are not just for entertainment
ut to break down the artificial barriers which separate people
rom each other—the mad from the sane, the schizophrenic
rom the non-schizophrenic.

Certain hospitals have set up *departments of voluntary service*
hrough which teams of volunteers are selected, trained and
upported while they come to work inside the hospital. This is

not just to set out flowers and to serve teas but to meet the patients in a real and personal way. Making meaningful contact with a volunteer may be the first step in the direction of leaving the hospital for good.

Community Treatment

Dr K. Myers, MB, BCh., DPM
Consultant Psychiatrist, Middlewood Hospital, Sheffield

One of the most important and exciting developments in the years since the Second World War has been the growth of social psychiatry; that is, the recognition of the importance of the environment, and especially the people in it, not only in the genesis of mental illness but also in its treatment. Obviously, such recognition has existed for a long time; in the moral treatment era of the last century due regard was paid to the importance of kindness, of occupation and of pleasant surroundings in creating the best sort of atmosphere for the care of the mentally ill. There has, too, long been due acknowledgement of the part that work, occupational therapy and different forms of group therapy can play in resocialising those handicapped by mental illness.

The significance of the development in social psychiatry in the last twenty years has, however, to a large extent been centred on the developments that have taken place in group therapy. Treatment in a group setting has been tried with small groups of people with neurotic disorders, with family groups and with psychopaths; the aim has been to help the participants to gain insight into the reasons for their symptoms and disturbed behaviour and to learn more realistic patterns of action. More recently, following the work of sociologists in psychiatric hospitals, it has been recognised that patients living together in a ward are, in fact, living in a discrete sma society with its own social structure, and attention ha deliberately been paid to using the existence of that society a part of the treatment programme.

Whereas in the traditional ward patients are seen a individuals with differing treatment needs, different back grounds and differing prognoses, in the ward in which th principles of social psychiatry are applied the patients are, *i addition*, seen as members of the ward society, interacting witl other patients and staff influencing and being influenced by them. Further, it is assumed that *all* patients and staff ar members of the ward society or community and all, even the most psychotic, can and do interact with others to some extent and can be influenced by them. To this extent, the ward community can be a therapeutic community. How therapeutic will depend on how much use is deliberately made of the human resources available.

In the typical therapeutic community all patients and staff meet daily, usually in the morning, to discuss the social events of the previous twenty-four hours, to receive reports from various small groups, to try to analyse and understand the upsets that inevitably occur during the working day of a hospital ward. Discussion is free and egalitarian and results in a realisation on the part of the staff that their traditional privilege of having the last word, or talking in a respectful silence, is not only liable to be challenged but that it *is* challenged; doctors find that in matters of nursing or the day-to-day minutiae of life on the ward they may have little to contribute, and they are told so in no uncertain terms. This in turn results in careful self-examination, in considerable attention being paid to each person's role, and this attitude also applies to the role each patient plays in the life of the ward community.

It follows that traditional roles become blurred, and that they may overlap; in the setting of the large ward meeting communication between patients and staff, and all levels and divisions of staff, is more direct. This, again, is in contrast to the traditional ward, where patients are at the bottom of a pyramid of communication, most of which occurs in a downward direction. This alteration of communication patterns will have a special significance for the schizophrenic patient, who has particular difficulties in communicating.

One of the features of life in a therapeutic community is the emphasis on reality. The schizophrenic who acts on delusions, whose behaviour is bizarre and unpredictable, who succeeds in annoying others or ignoring them completely, is confronted with what he is doing. This can happen at any time, but most frequently in the setting of a ward meeting, where all involved are present. This reality confrontation makes use of the assumption, already referred to, that everybody is to some extent responsible for his actions; that *he* is the best person to regulate or control them; that realisation of his effect on others together with an understanding of their reactions to him is the best approach to improved interpersonal relations.

This emphasis on reality is seen in meetings, certainly, but also in social gatherings and working situations, both of which are deliberately arranged to provide a series of settings in which the patient can function in a variety of ways, with development of the ability to relate to others in a variety of roles. For example, the schizophrenic patient may be encouraged to attend at the hospital industrial unit daily, where, for a regular wage, he does a useful job.

There are several advantages to be gained. First, he earns money. Then, he develops the habit of regular work and regular hours of working. But, certainly of great importance, he also learns to play the role of worker in relation to his companions at the bench: he has to relate to the foreman or supervisor in a realistic way, without delusional or suspicious overtones. He has to be aware that he has a measure of responsibility as a member of a working team; and he learns that, whatever delusions, hallucinations or impulses he suffers from, to bring them to work and respond to them can only result in discomfort or even disaster for himself.

In social gatherings there is another set of roles to be

learned. He learns to relate to people as social equals, i
settings where the overt goal is enjoyment by all participating
Ordinary social graces, politeness, thoughtfulness of others
good manners are the goals aimed at. Relating to other
without being suspicious of them, without upsetting or bein
upset by them, is the desirable end for most schizophrenics
Thus, ward parties, shopping expeditions, visits to the cinema
fund-raising projects, dances all become part of social treat
ment.

In the therapeutic community there are limitations set o
disturbed, disturbing and bizarre behaviour by the sanction
imposed by the community itself, discussing together th
steps to be taken. For example, after a particularly disturbe
period the community may advise that a patient is not wel
enough to spend a weekend at home. It is legitimate for them
to do so because they live in close proximity to one anothe
for most of the twenty-four hours, and have more knowledge
of day-to-day happenings than anyone else. On the other hand
positive sanctions exist too; encouragement of periods o
leave can occur, and the social treatment itself—the partie
and outings—can carry its own rewards.

Therapeutic community treatment makes demands, emo
tional and physical, on those involved in it, both on patient
and staff. It can be exhausting, and not everybody can tolerat
it. But it is rewarding for those who can tolerate uncertainty.
who want to see treatment in which everybody can contribute
and which, for the schizophrenic, breaks the vicious circle o
withdrawal, rejection and withdrawal again.

Community Support

K. D. Armitage
Senior Social Worker, Social Services Department,
Cambridgeshire North Area

With the changing emphasis of caring for the mentally disordered in the community, we have seen in recent years a
decided strengthening of the relationship between Local
Authority Social Workers in Mental Health and their col-
leagues in the hospital Psychiatric Service. No legislation has
been necessary to achieve this co-operation, which has come
about with the realisation that much more could be done for
the patient by pooling the resources, knowledge and facilities
at our disposal. Hospital doctors, Local Authority Medical
Officers of Health and General Practitioners have done a
great deal to encourage flexibility, and the team approach to
the problem of schizophrenia has to some extent prevented
the psychiatric hospitals being overburdened with long-term
chronic patients.

The following outlines some of the developments which
have helped the schizophrenic patient to be contained within
the community.

A place to live

Often the family of a hospitalised schizophrenic may well be
totally opposed to him rejoining them. This attitude, histori-
cally based on fear and ignorance, no longer should apply.

Relatives Groups are being formed whereby contact with the supportive agencies is readily available and advice on management within the home environment is freely given.

Some research has shown that schizophrenics on the whole do better if they do not go back to families where high demands are made of them, but are placed in accommodation where the emotional atmosphere is less tense and the patient can progress at his own speed.

Where there is no home or relatives, the social worker can prepare a list of *suitable lodgings* with sympathetic landladies, with whom some time has been spent in explanation of the patient's difficulties and future plans. Some local authorities already have excellent *boarding-out schemes*; others are providing suitable Hostels and Group Homes. Local voluntary societies have done an immense amount of good work in initiating these projects, and the success rate is most encouraging.

A hostel is run by a Warden and Matron and several models may be used, ranging from a strictly organised authoritarian structure, in which the resident is encouraged to lean on the staff for help, to houses run on therapeutic community lines, in which the resident is encouraged to find out sources for his own help.

A *Group Home* usually has no resident staff but is visited once a week by a social worker. The residents live together in bed-sitters and can be as independent of each other as they wish.

The Hostels and Group Homes provide a useful halfway house between being in hospital and being completely independent out in the community.

A place to work

Some psychiatric hospitals hold regular *Resettlement Clinics* where patients are interviewed prior to their discharge from hospital. The Disabled Resettlement Officer (DRO) from the Department of Employment and Productivity usually attends, along with medical, nursing, occupational therapy and social worker representatives, with a view to planning a realistic future for the patient. Various recommendations can be made.

Attendance at an *Industrial Rehabilitation Unit* (IRU) may be appropriate, depending on the skill and the potential of the patient. Unfortunately, these units are small in number and there is a waiting time for admission. The patient attends for about six weeks and is put through a variety of assessment procedures, including tests by an Industrial Psychologist. At the end of the course a full assessment report is made which will suggest one of the following:

(*a*) The patient is not yet fit for employment.
(*b*) The patient has skill to offer in the open employment market.
(*c*) The patient requires further training which he can receive at a *Government Training Centre* (GTC), a course lasting up to six to nine months. After this he can be placed in open employment.

Many local authorities have provided *workshop places* for the schizophrenic patient who is able to work under sheltered conditions. Subcontracting from local industrial concerns enables the workshops to provide useful and meaningful employment or a retraining in industrial practices. To a lesser degree, the *Adult Training Centre* for the subnormal can provide an appropriate setting for selected schizophrenic patients with limited skills.

Sympathetic employers, often few and far between, can and do provide employment suitable to the psychologically disabled patient. Simple and repetitive processes, normally shunned by ordinary people, can be adequately performed. This often calls for close co-operation between the employer and the social worker to meet the inevitable crises, but these are largely overcome by a sensible and understanding approach. It should be understood, however, that with modern industrial practices changing so rapidly machinery is taking over these simple jobs and, therefore, we may well in the future have to revise our provision of *sheltered workshops* as a place where the schizophrenic can work within his limita tions.

As a further development, hostels are being set up in asso ciation with sheltered workshops so that the selected patien can be totally independent of an otherwise hospital-based existence.

A place to socialise

An essential part of the schizophrenic's rehabilitation starts during the period of treatment. Most psychiatric hospitals provide a social club for patients where contact with other people is established. A period of relearning the art of social ising in a realistic way is most valuable, especially if this is carried forward to the *Social Clubs* which many local authori ties and voluntary agencies provide. Patients are encouraged to take the responsibility of organising the clubs themselves with a minimum support and dependence on authority figures.

Day Centres which provide social, therapeutic and treatment facilities are slowly developing into an integral part of the overall pattern of treatment of the schizophrenic patient.

Community Centres and *Youth Groups* are opening their doors to the younger patients, allowing them to participate in everyday, normal situations with normal people. The younger generation appears to be able to accept and understand the less fortunate members of society more easily than their elders. In this way, the process of reintegration into society and accept ance of former patients is developed. With more schizophrenic patients spending more time out of hospitals, society is becoming accustomed to their limitations and showing more tolerance of their presence.

The stigma of having been mad is a very real one and hard to overcome for both patients and friends, but social contacts go a long way to dispel the doubts and apprehensions which lie behind this phenomenon.

A place for urgent help

A most important aspect of the supportive work with a schizophrenic patient is accessibility to the General Practitioner and to the Psychiatric Out-patient Clinic. With the development of the *Community Health Centre*, the Psychiatrist, General Practitioner and the Social Worker in Mental Health can ideally meet at least weekly. In this way, most crisis situations with the schizophrenic patient can be discussed and immediate action taken. Crisis resolution is all very well, but rather the old adage that 'Prevention is better than cure'.

Many social workers in mental health have regular supportive clinics weekly in larger towns, and along with the general practitioners are visiting the more isolated patients in their homes at regular intervals. The domiciliary nursing service are also taking a more active part in the preventative field of mental health and are part of an effective 'early-warning' system.

Community education in matters of mental health plays an increasing part in advising neighbours, friends and relatives on how they can be of use in giving practical help and understanding to a mentally disturbed person. In recent years we have seen the growth of '*good neighbour*' schemes, and selected *volunteers* are supporting the statutory services by visiting patients, offering practical help, baby-sitting, providing transport and assistance at social clubs. Schizophrenics need no longer live in isolation, tormented by fears and detached from reality.

The community has indeed extended a helping hand to them, both in the hospitals and in their homes.

Postscript

Throughout this book a number of themes have emerged from the consideration of madness which have important implications for us all. They help us to avoid the separatism and the division of experience into 'us' and 'them' which lies behind so much of the world's ills at the present time, and generates so much anxiety, hostility and paranoia. Madness is universal ('all the world's queer except me and thee, and tha's a bit queer at times') and madness is protective ('the mad are the only truly sane, for they have opted out of our crazy world'). Before we are quick to condemn or to reject the mad, it is as well to bear these implications in mind.

1 Madness is not something that happens to other people—it can and does happen to us all.
2 The mad are not foreign creatures, but they are ourselves, lost in a maze from which there seems at the time to be no escape.
3 We all become 'mad' at times—mad with anger, with fear, with pain, with grief; for a time we are crazy and gone out of our minds.
4 It is a comfort for us to be able to class others as mad, for it is only then that we are able to class ourselves as sane.
5 We all have an entry into the world of madness through

intoxicants and nightmares, and through the means by which the forces of the deep unconscious come out into consciousness, as in dreams, art, superstition and mythology. We live in a mad world where man is the only creature that makes war on his own kind and destroys his own species. The concentration camps, nuclear warfare and witch hunts (both historical and political) are as much the faces of madness as the poor lunatic singing his sweet songs to the pallid moon. We all walk through the human jungle where there is a primitive struggle for survival of the self, which ultimately means the destruction, or at least the disadvantaging, of others.

'Like madness is the glory of this life.'

'And what shall it profit a man
If he gain the whole world, but lose his own soul?'

Glossary

Technical terms used in the text

Affect   Feeling, emotion, desire.

Autism   Condition in which the subject appears to have lost contact with reality and is absorbed in fantasy.

Catatonic   Fixed, rigid, in a frozen state.

Catharsis   The release and expression of pent-up emotion.

Cephalopod   Human figure seen in schizophrenic art (literally, 'head—foot').

Chromosome   Staining thread in the nucleus which carries the **Genes** (*q.v.*).

Cognitive   Concerned with thinking and knowing.

Constitution   That aspect of the organism which is compounded of hereditary and accumulated experience.

Covert   That which is hidden and disguised.

Delusion   A false unshakeable belief.

Depersonalisation   Feeling of loss of contact with oneself, loss of personal wholeness.

Diagnosis   The scientific process of ascertaining and determining the nature of an illness.

ECT   Electroconvulsant therapy   A form of physical treatment inducing controlled fits.

EEG   Electroencephalogram   Tracing of the electrical activity of the brain.

Ego   Awareness of self, conscious identity.

Epilepsy Organic disorder characterised by episodic cerebral discharges (fits).

Existential That branch of philosophy or psychology concerned with the nature of being.

Functional Involving the function of an organism rather than its structure (see **Organic**).

Gene Packet of inherited material which controls cell behaviour and growth.

Gestalt An organised whole, consisting of figure and background.

Hallucination A false perception in the absence of a stimulus (see **Illusion**).

Hallucinogen A chemical substance which causes hallucinations.

Hebephrenia Variant of schizophrenia, fatuous madness of the young.

Hypnagogic Pertaining to that period just before the onset of sleep.

Hysteria A neurotic condition characterised by dissociation.

Illusion Mistaken perception in the presence of a stimulus (see **Hallucination**).

Insanity Legal connotation of madness.

Leucotomy A brain operation in which white matter (nerve tracts) is severed.

Lunacy Archaic use, implying madness due to an effect of the moon.

Madness State of being out of one's mind.

Metabolism The chemical processes of the body.

Neologism Personally created word (literally 'new word').

Neurosis Minor form of psychiatric illness, principally affecting the emotions.

Non mens rea Not being in one's right mind (legal).

Organic Involving the structure of the body or its chemical processes (see **Functional**).

Overt That which is open and apparent.

Paranoid Suspicious, with delusions of grandeur or persecution.

Phenomenology Branch of science which studies the nature of experience.

Prognosis Scientific process of predicting the outcome of an illness.

Psychiatry Branch of medicine which studies disorders of the mind.

Psychic Pertaining to the mind (see **Somatic**).

Psychoanalysis Psychological technique using free association to reveal unconscious material.

Psychodrama A psychological treatment which uses the acting out of defined roles.

Psychology Branch of science which studies behaviour.

Puerperium Period immediately following childbirth.

Rapport Feeling of relationship, togetherness and communication.

Rorschach The projective ink blot test.

Schizoid A type of personality, introspective and preferring objects to persons.

Schizophrenia Special forms of madness, in which the mind is divided against itself.

Schizophreniform Having some of the qualities of schizophrenia, schizophrenia-like.

Schizophrenogenic Rendering someone liable to become schizophrenic.

Somatic Pertaining to the body (see **Psychic**).

Somatotype Classification of body configuration.

Unconscious That part of the mind not available to conscious processes.

Who's Who

Medical authorities mentioned in the text

Aesculapius (1250 BC): Greek God of Healing.

Hippocrates (fifth century BC): Father of Medicine and founder of the Hippocratean School of Medicine.

Andreas Vesalius (sixteenth century): foremost anatomist of the Renaissance.

Anton Mesmer (eighteenth century): Viennese practitioner who invented 'animal magnetism'.

James Braid (nineteenth century): Scots physician who first coined the term 'hypnotism'.

Sigmund Freud (1856–1939): the father of psychological psychiatry and the founder of psychoanalysis.

Joseph Breuer (1842–1925): contemporary of Freud's who worked with him on hysteria.

Pierre Janet (1859–1947): contemporary of Freud's who worked with him on dissociation.

Jean-Martin Charcot (1825–1893): great French neurologist who practised at the Salpetriéré Hospital in Paris.

Ivan Pavlov (1849–1936): Russian neuro-psychologist who developed the theory of conditioned learning.

Hans Berger contemporary neuro-physiologist who first displayed the EEG in 1929.

Emil Kraepelin (1855–1936): great German psychiatric systematiser.

Eugen Bleuler: contemporary German/Swiss psychiatrist who first used the term schizophrenia in 1911.

R. D. Laing: contemporary British phenomenological psychiatrist.

Gregory Bateson: contemporary American sociologist who invented the Double Bind theory.

Further Reading

Psychiatry Today, David Stafford Clark (Pelican Books: A262)

A Dictionary of Psychology, James Drever (Penguin Reference Book: R5)

Schizophrenia: The Divided Mind, Joyce Emerson (Family Doctor/National Association for Mental Health joint publication)

Schizophrenia, Frank Fish (John Wright & Sons Ltd, 1962)

The Psychology of Insanity, Bernard Hart (Cambridge University Press, 1962)

New Horizons in Psychiatry, Peter Hays (Pelican Books)

The Divided Self, R. D. Laing (Pelican Books: A734)

The Self and Others, R. D. Laing (Tavistock Publications, London 1961)

Sanity, Madness and the Family, R. D. Laing and A. Esterson (Pelican Books)

Student Casualties, Anthony Ryle (Allen Lane: Penguin Press, 1969)

Portrait of a Schizophrenic Nurse, Clare Marc Wallace (Hammond and Company, 1965)

To Define True Madness, Henry Yellowlees (Pelican Books: A3357)

Index

Index